The Woodruffs Of New Jersey Who Came From Fordwich, Kent, England, By Way Of Lynn, Massachusetts, And Southampton, Long Island...

Francis Eben Woodruff

THE WOODRUFFS
OF NEW JERSEY

*Compliments of the
Author*

THE WOODRUFFS
OF NEW JERSEY

The Woodruffs of New Jersey

By Francis E. Woodruff
of Morristown, N. J.

The Grafton Press, Publishers, 70 Fifth Ave., N. Y.,

THIS is a revised and enlarged edition of "A Branch of the Woodruff Stock" published in pamphlet form some time ago. Its most important feature is the connecting, for the first time, of the immigrant ancestor, John Woodruff, with his forebears of the town of Fordwich, Kent, England. Towards this a learned and courteous English cousin has greatly aided, by clinching the proof of the connection and by, through his previous researches and publications, carrying the line up to the year 1508, when Thomas Woodrove, then a man grown, was its representative at Fordwich.

For the general readers of the family there are five sketches, telling of the lives of the members of the male line. Something is said of the earlier generations at quaint little Fordwich, until, in 1638, Mr. Gosmer,—who had married the widowed mother of the immigrant (John Woodruff),—as Mayor of that town resisted King Charles' illegal exaction of ship-money, in 1639 had warning, and in 1640 appeared, with his family, in America.

Next we read of Southampton, L. I., with its whaling squadron, land division and political vicissitudes until, in the latter half of the 17th century, the two sons John of the immigrant John Woodruff became the progenitors, respectively, of the Elizabeth branch and (through a son Joseph) of the West-field branch of the New Jersey family. The further history of the former branch is left to the care of its members. The Westfield Joseph, having been the defendant in the famous Vaughan ejectment suit, brings in the story of the long struggle between the "Elizabeth Town Associates" and the "Proprietors of East Jersey". Then came the revolutionary war, and modern times.

The Sketches are followed by full Notes for genealogists. The Appendix also, is made up of miscellaneous genealogical matter, such as a record of descendants of Dr. H. S. Woodruff (Generation IX); more about those who lived at Westfield; and notes on the lineage of the families of the maternal ancestors. One of the latter,—that on the Coursens of Sussex County, N. J., —is more considerable than the others, and is reprinted as well in a separate booklet. It carries the family up from 1763 to 1649 when its representative was at Recife (Brazil), then in the possesion of Holland; through which country it is hoped, other hands will carry it to the traditional home in France.

There is an old-fashioned index (names of persons, places and subjects) that is accurate and fairly complete. Ten half-tone illustrations (four of them maps) give an idea of the life in Fordwich, Southampton, Westfield and Morris County, N. J.

Both are octavos, bound in cloth and printed on Grafton all rag paper.

ORDER BLANK

To GRAFTON PRESS
          70 Fifth Avenue, New York

          Please send me by   Express charges collect,
the following:

          .. copies The Woodruffs of New Jersey at $5.00 net
              "   The Coursens   -   -   at $1.00 net

Enclosed find   for $ in payment.

If you remit by check, add 10 cents for collection charge.

PLATE A.—FORDWICH FROM THE STONE BRIDGE.

Reproduced by permission from "The History of Fordwich."

(See Note 4.)

HE WOODRUFF
OF NEW JERSEY

FORDWICH, K

MASSACHU

HAMPTON, LONG ISLAN

FROM

WOODRUFF

Life Member of *New York*
istorical Socie *New Jersey*

E GRAFTON PRESS

GICAL PUBLISHERS

MCMIX

...H FROM THE STONE BRIDGE.

...n from "The History of ...odwich"

(See Note 4.)

THE WOODRUFFS
OF NEW JERSEY

WHO CAME FROM FORDWICH, KENT, ENGLAND, BY WAY OF LYNN, MASSACHUSETTS, AND SOUTHAMPTON, LONG ISLAND

REVISED AND ENLARGED FROM
"A BRANCH OF THE WOODRUFF STOCK"

BY

FRANCIS E. WOODRUFF, B.A. (YALE, 1864)

Life Member of the New Jersey Historical Society, New York Historical Society, and Washington Association of New Jersey

THE GRAFTON PRESS

GENEALOGICAL PUBLISHERS

NEW YORK   MCMIX

CONTENTS

ILLUSTRATIONS

PREFACE

THESE papers were originally intended for the "Proceedings of the New Jersey Historical Society," and Sketch I appeared in No. 1 of Part III, Third Series, September, 1898, page 36; but the issue of the "Proceedings" having been temporarily suspended, the writer, to keep rash promises of sending copies, with the Society's consent, published them in leaflet form.

A very little research made plain to the beginner that their chosen title, "A Branch of The Woodruff Stock," is misleading; "A Branch of A Woodruff Stock" would be nearer the mark. For in the day of "wood-reeves" (Woodreeve-Woodruff, Note 14) there were presumably some scores at least of men not closely related to each other who were alike known as "——— the Woodreeve," and of these doubtless some have been followed down to date by unbroken male lines of descendants, which thus, while bearing similar surnames, are yet of different "Woodruff" stocks. So the title substituted in this revised edition in book form seems preferable.

Warned by finding hard and good genealogical and historical work made largely unavailable, or even altogether useless, by death, the writer has attempted no more than the laying of foundations he could complete in his lifetime, and so leave in such shape that others could build on them. He hopes, as stated in the Note to Appendix B, that all of the descendants of John Woodruffe, 1604-70, of Southampton, Long Island, will similarly make sure that a record for their immediate families is compiled and the result sent to The New Jersey Historical Society's "Woodruff Collection" (to be), in readiness for the coming genealogist, who will weave the separate records into a comprehensive history.

At the beginning, while writing for the more limited space of a periodical, thanks deeply felt were not fully expressed to Mr. Pelletreau and the others; but now are to all who have so kindly helped the writer in his work. The labor has brought him much pleasure, both from their kindliness, and from the many evidences during his visits to the former homes of his people that they are still held in warm remembrance.

F. E. W.

MORRISTOWN, NEW JERSEY, January, 1909.

ABBREVIATIONS AND AUTHORITIES

E.; Etown. Elizabeth (Town), New Jersey.

Early Germans. The Early Germans of New Jersey, by Theodore Frelinghuysen Chambers, 1895.

E. L. I. W. Early Long Island Wills of Suffolk County: 1691-1703, with notes by Wm. S. Pelletreau, A.M. 1897.

Gen. Generation.

Hatfield. History of Elizabeth, New Jersey. By Rev. Edwin F. Hatfield, D.D. 1868.

Heitman. Historical Register of Officers of the Continental Army during the War of the Revolution. April, 1775, to December, 1783. By B. F. Heitman. 1893.

Hist. County History.

Howell. The Early History of Southampton, L. I. By George Rogers Howell, M.A. (Yale). 2d Ed., 1887.

Ill. Illustration.

Inscriptions. Inscriptions on Tombstones and Monuments in the Burying Grounds of The First Presbyterian Church and St. John's Church at Elizabeth, New Jersey, 1664, 1892. By Wm. Ogden Wheeler and Edmund D. Halsey. 1892.

Littell. Family Records; or Genealogies of the First Settlers of Passaic Valley (and vicinity). Above Chatham—with their Ancestors and Descendants. As far as can now be ascertained. By John Littell. 1851.

M. Married.

Mor. Morris County, New Jersey.

Register. History of the First Presbyterian Church, Morristown, N. J. Part II. The Combined Register, from 1742 to 1885.

So.; S. Southampton, Long Island.

S. T. R. Records of the Town of Southampton (printed 1874-96).

S. T. R. W. S. P. Same, Mr. William S. Pelletreau's Introduction and Notes.

S. T. R. Orig. Same, Original Records at Southampton.

Stryker. Official Register of the Officers and Men of New Jersey
   in the Revolutionary War. William S. Stryker, Adjutant-
   General. 1872.

T. Trenton, New Jersey.

Thompson. History of Long Island, etc., etc., etc. By Benjamin
   F. Thompson, etc., New York. 1839.

W. Westfield, New Jersey.

Wickes. History of Medicine in New Jersey, and of Medical Men
   of the State. From the Settlement of the Province to 1800.
   By Stephen Wickes, A.M., M.D. 1879.

Winans. Professor Samuel Ross Winans (Ph.D.), Princeton University.

N.B.—The notes following the five Sketches are numbered consecutively, and are referred to by their numbers instead of being
repeated.

THE WOODRUFFS OF NEW JERSEY

MALE LINE

DOUBTLESS in this State there are descendants of Matthew Woodruff,[20] of Farmington, Connecticut, and even of other Woodruffs (Preface), with none of whom we descendants of John Woodruff (Sketch II), of Southampton, Long Island, have any known family connection; but we so overwhelmingly outnumber them in the State that we may be forgiven for calling ourselves "The Woodruffs of New Jersey."

THE GENERATIONS

    I.   Thomas Woodrove, Fordwich, 1508-1552.
   II.   William Woodroffe, Fordwich, died 1587.
  III.   Robert Woodroffe, Fordwich, died 1611.
  IV.   John Woodroffe, I, Fordwich, 1574-1611.
   V.   John Woodruffe, II, Fordwich, Southampton, 1604-1670.
  VI.   John Woodruff, III, E.; Southampton, Etown, 1637-1691.
        (Succession left for Etown descendants to fill in.)
  VI.   John Woodruffe, III, So.; Southampton, 1650-1703.
 VII.   Joseph Woodruffe, Southampton, Westfield, 1676-1742.
VIII.   Hezekiah Woodruff, Westfield, 1724-1776.
  IX.   Hezekiah Stites Woodruff, Westfield, Morris county, 1754-1842.
        (N.B.—Succession of writer's immediate family.)
   X.   Absalom Woodruff, Morris county, 1791-1850.
  XI.   Ebenezer Blachly Woodruff, Succasunna, Morristown, 1814-1885.
 XII.   Edward Coursen Woodruff, I, Morristown, Glen Ridge, living.
XIII.   Edward Coursen Woodruff, II, Glen Ridge, living.

I

MR. JOHN GOSMER

MR. JOHN GOSMER

MR. JOHN GOSMER,[1] when "Mr." was reserved for the few, was one of the founders of Southampton, Long Island. His name at first attracted the attention of the writer because he was the stepfather (not father-in-law, as we have long believed)[2] of our ancestor John Woodruff, the immigrant; but acquaintance with his career quickly made him interesting for himself.

As Howell[3] has told us, he came (as did John Woodruff) from Fordwich (see frontispiece), in Kent, England, a quaint little town situated on the right bank of the river Stour, once far-famed for its delicious sea-trout, two or three miles below the city of Canterbury, of which, in the long ago, it was the port. For now an inland village, in Saxon days it was at the head of a tidal estuary; so the early Kentish kings made it a customs station, whose commercial importance declined as silt made the river less navigable.

It was the "little burgh which is called Forewic," when the Domesday survey was made in the year 1085. Later it became a member of the Cinque Ports' confederacy. Some time between the years 1218 and 1292 it obtained full corporate privileges (a list of its annually elected mayors, beginning with the latter year, has, with much labor, been compiled from the existing records); but for centuries its burgesses had to struggle for their rights against the encroachments of their ecclesiastical and other overlords. As the times changed, and Fordwich became a mere hamlet, the governing body gradually outlived its usefulness. Finally, by the Municipal Reforms Act of 1883, it ceased to be "at once the smallest and one of the oldest of the Kentish municipalities."

What the writer has just told about Fordwich, and is to tell about the Gosmer and Woodruff families, he owes to the Reverends A. M. Chichester, R. Hitchcock, and C. E. Woodruff, of Kent; but chiefly to the latter, to whom, for his most valuable history of Fordwich,[4] memorials of the Fordwich Woodruffs,[5] and courteous help, all New Jersey Woodruffs are very deeply indebted.

5

If we may judge from the records, Mr. Gosmer was the first of his line in Fordwich; but whether he came from some other part of England, or from the Continent, has still to be ascertained. The earliest occurrence of his name that has been found is the signature of John Gozmur as witness to a will (proved in Oct., 1611) of a John Woodruffe, of the parish of St. Marie's of Northgate (adjoining Fordwich[6]), who named in it his wife Elizabeth and young son John, our immigrant ancestor. The times were so stormy that women and children must have protection, and Oct. 24, 1611, John Gosmore was married to Elizabeth Woodruffe, widow (both being of the parish of St. Mary, Northgate[7]). He thus became the stepfather of our ancestor.

In 1613, John Gosmer, sidesman (churchwarden's assistant), signed (after the vicar and churchwardens) a bill of "Christenings, Marriages, and Burials in the Parish of St. Mary, Northgate." In 1618, John Gosmer, bachelor, joiner, of St. Mary Northgate, married Ann Woodruff, widow.[8] As after much kind research no other Gosmer items prior to this year 1618 have been found in the records, whether Mr. John Gosmer was a widower when he married the widow Elizabeth, and whether he was the father by a first wife of the John Gosmer of 1618, and, as has been suggested, of the Anne who married our ancestor John Woodruff, are matters of conjecture.

In 1637 it is recorded[4] that there was a dispute between the Fordwich Corporation and Mr. Gosmer (as a tenant of the Chapter of Canterbury) regarding the extent of their respective rights over some land; which was referred to arbitration. The result is not known to us, but in 1638 Mr. Gosmer was himself the Mayor of the Corporation.[4] All England was then in the throes of the impending civil war, and, like other ports, Fordwich resisted King Charles' illegal exaction of ship-money. In 1639 the Council in Whitehall demanded from Mr. Gosmer's successor in the mayoralty the unpaid assessment for 1638, "which should long since have been paid to the Sheriff of Kent or the Treasurer of the Navy."[4] We know that in 1640 a Mr. Gosmer was in America.

Efforts made at Sandwich (a port just seaward of Fordwich) and Dover in England, and in the United States, have failed to find any record of his emigration. The item may possibly be buried in the unexamined manuscripts of the Public Record Office of England; but Hotten[9] in his Introduction says in effect that only the names of those emigrants were taken who legally left the shores of England; that those who went (as Mr. Gosmer obviously did) to avoid payment of the hated ship-money left secretly; and that of such no record would exist.

Be all this as it may, so far as the writer can ascertain there has never been but this one John Gosmer in America; and, with the added authority of Howell (2 Ed., p. 427) there can be no reasonable doubt that it was the ex-Mayor of Fordwich who is next on record[10] at Lynn, Massachusetts, where already, on March 10, 1639, the founding of Southampton, Long Island, had been formally "undertaken." By the mutilated declaration of the Company we know that on the 4th day of the 4th—16—(probably June 4, 1640), "Mr. John Gosmere" was "admitted an undertaker." At Southampton, on Dec. 16, 1640, the name of "Mr. John Gosmer" headed the list of the parties of the second part to the "Indian Deed" for the land lying eastward "between the foresaid bounds by water" from the place "where the Indians hayle their cannoes out of the North Bay to the southside of the Island," later known as Canoe Place.[10]

On March 7, 1644, it was ordered that "yf by the providence of God there shall be henceforth within the bounds of this plantacon any whale or whales cast up," certain designated townsmen should attend to their "cutting out." In this; in dealing with the Shinnecocks, Montauks and other tribes; in dividing the lands among the townsmen; in fencing out the wilderness; in clearing off the forests; and in all the varied tasks of a new settlement, the town records show that "John Gosmer, Gentleman," took a leading part. For the enforcement of law and order, magistrates (generally three in number) were elected by the General Court (town meeting), "who were looked upon with a degree of veneration that the modern occupants of the office can hardly hope to obtain";[10] in 1644 he was already a magistrate. When, in 1647, Southampton entered into a compact with Connecticut, Mr. Edward Howell and he were the first to represent the town in the House of Magistrates in the General Court at Hartford; and he continued to serve until 1650.[11]

Then, in the midst of his prosperity, a lifelong grief came to him in the death of his only son, Richard, whose estate he administered in the year 1650.[10] As on March 7, 1644, the son had been appointed to the whaling squadron[10], his presumable age at that time indicates that he was born in England; and as he was appointed from the 3d Ward, while his father was appointed from the 2d Ward, he presumably had a house of his own. Notwithstanding this, Howell says that he appears to have died unmarried; and, whether married or not, that his father adopted a son, and that the name of Gosmer dropped out of the record after the death of the survivor, must seem sufficient evidence that he died without leaving male issue.

In 1652 Mr. Gosmer was the *Primus* of the three Southampton magistrates; and he was re-elected several years in succession.[10] During 1655-1658 he again represented his town at Hartford.[11] When, in 1657, there was an Indian alarm, and "for preservation of ye towne" it was voted that all men should "lay downe themselves in respect of their persons & estates, to bee disposed of by the said 7 men in a way of righteousness, to attend any means that may in their Judgement effect the said ends," he was one of the seven.[3][10]

Already, however, he had begun to set his house in order. In 1655 he bought property in Boston, which in 1658 he made over "to his kinswoman, Ann, widow of Richard Carter."[12] In 1657 his stepson, John Woodruff, succeeded him in the whaling squadron. It is probably in the same year that this John Woodruff, Sr., received from him the "messuage or tenement over against the said Mr. Gosmer his home lot, which said tenement he bought of John Topping" (in 1657), and "five acres of land"; though the deed was not recorded until Feb. 20, 1660-1. On July 29, 1659, he deeded to his "adopted sonne, who hath lived with me from a child, all my goods and chattells, house and lands"; to which Elizabeth his wife consented.[10] No other will has been found.

Then (after the entry of Feb. 20, 1660-61), he was lost from the town records that had so often shown him a masterful man of affairs, upright, able, energetic, wealthy, dignified, perhaps just a little bit dictatorial. In his "Puritan Settlers" Hinman has written: "an examination of the Colony records of Connecticut shows that Hon. John Gosmer, Mr. Edward Howell, Mr. John Ogden, Mr. Young, Captain Thomas Toppin, Thomas Baker and Robert Bond, were the leading men in the eastern half of Long Island in its early settlement." Doubtless, John Gosmer lies with his fellow pioneers in the old South End burying ground at Southampton; but their tombstones have crumbled into dust,[3] and, less fortunate than others, he has left no descendants of his name to remind men of a most worthy life. It rests with the descendants of the stepson to keep his memory green.

II

JOHN WOODRUFF, THE IMMIGRANT

JOHN WOODRUFF, THE IMMIGRANT

In the year 1508,[13] just at the end of the reign of King Henry VII, THOMAS WOODROVE[14] was the first of our name to appear in the records of the Kentish town of Fordwich (Sketch I[3 4]); the entry having been to note payment to the churchwardens of the rent of his house, due to the church for the preceding year, he was evidently then a man grown. That, increasing in age, he became a considerable property holder, is indicated by a deed of 1538 (Fordwich Muniments Chest, 9th, Henry VIII) recording Thomas Woderoff's ownership of 2 messuages, with 3 gardens, 30 acres of arable land, 5 acres of meadow, and 8 acres of wood, in Fordwich.

As has been told,[4 13] the Abbot of St. Augustine's Monastery, outside the walls of Canterbury, was Lord of the Manor of Fordwich, and claimed many rights within the Liberty (Borough) which were at variance with what the Mayor and Commonalty considered to be their chartered privileges. One obnoxious claim to which they had to submit was that the Abbot's bailiff must be present whenever the Mayor held court; and it was to summon a non-resident bailiff from his home that, in 1510, our ancestor was despatched with all speed to the neighboring Isle of Thanet. A few years after he rode on a longer, and in those days a more hazardous, journey, with a therefore needed companion, to Westminster, that, as trusted envoy of the town, he might pay a fine incurred by his fellow townsmen into the King's exchequer. Because in later days such duties were almost invariably intrusted to the town clerk, while there was then no office with that title, he was probably acting in that capacity. If so, it would have been in the line of promotion that he was a Jurat[15] in 1538, when, during Henry VIII's suppression of the greater monasteries, St. Augustine's estates were given over to the rapacity of the King and his courtiers. In the following year Thomas Woodrove sat with his fellow magistrates at Fordwich to arrange for the conveyancing to the favored courtiers of a portion of the possessions

11

of those against whom the Liberty had so long struggled for its privileges.

No other "Woodruff" was recorded until the mention (1550) in the Town Books of his son William. Shortly after this the name of Thomas disappeared from the records, his death occurring about 1552.

WILLIAM WOODROFFE, "the elder" (so called to distinguish him from his son William), died in 1587, when Elizabeth was Queen. During his lifetime Fordwich, now freed from the restrictions imposed by the Abbot of St. Augustine's, was encouraged to rebuild its Court Hall, and the unpretentious little building of timber and plaster, on the banks of the Stour, remains to-day[4][13] (it appears in the frontispiece, on the hither side of the church) in much the same condition, both outwardly and inwardly, as when it was completed in 1555. William took an active part in municipal affairs, and became a Jurat.[15] From his generally signing the minutes of the Court, he apparently presided, perhaps as senior Jurat, in the frequent absences of the Mayor. He was also a "Key Keeper of the Town Chest," a very honorable office conferred upon "the two best men of the Liberty."[13] The "Chest" (one of its representatives is shown in illustration B) was for the safe custody of deeds and other important records, fees being charged for the service. There is little further mention of him in the annals other than the entry in the Fordwich muster roll of 1573 that "Willyam Wodruf thelder wt his men Robert Woodrufe and Edward Parker wt his furniture" is credited with "one calyver furnyshed one almon rivett furnyshed."[4] (The caliver was a handgun that was fired from the shoulder, the heavier musket of that day requiring a rest; "alman-rivetts," a sort of light, flexible armor, of German origin.) The Mayor and seven others preceded him on the roll, twenty-one followed.

Besides the son Robert above, his son William was also on the roll; of their respective families, that of William became extinct in 1673, when the grandson, Thomas, died without issue.

ROBERT WOODROFFE, from whose day our descent can be verified by the parish register as well as by the town records, figured, as did his brother William, in the Town Books as a freeman (entitled to the privileges of the Borough); and is on record as a Jurat[15] and a Churchwarden (1584). He married, 1572, Alice Russell, of the parish of St. Mary Northgate,[6] had children, John and William, and died in 1611, when James I reigned. His son,

JOHN WOODRUFFE, born in 1574, on coming to man's estate took up his residence in Northgate,[6] where his uncle, William Russell,

Plate B.—A Corner of the Court Hall.

was a churchwarden. He married, 1601, Elizabeth Cartwright; their son John was baptized in 1604; in 1611 he died, at the early age of thirty-seven. His will "would not lead us to suppose that any increase to his fortune had resulted from his removal to Northgate." In it, "delivered this (sic) of September, 1611," when he was "very sick in bodye," and proved in October, 1611, he, "John Woodruffe," "husbandman" (head of a household), bade that he "be buried at the direction of my well-beloved wyffe"; named minor legacies to his young and only son John, and others; and left all the rest of his "goods and chattills" to his wife Elizabeth. The widow married Mr. John Gosmer[7].

This thorough search through the records by the Rev. C. Eveleigh Woodruff has shown that so far back as 1508 our ancestors were freemen of Fordwich[4] and men of standing in the community. Apparently they were Kentish yeomen[16] of, to judge from the surname, Saxon blood. Later discovered records and further researches may some time carry us back to a still earlier day.

JOHN WOODRUFFE, baptized 1604, only son of John Woodruffe, 1574-1611, of St. Mary Northgate, having by the remarriage[7] of his mother, Elizabeth, become the stepson of Mr. John Gosmer, of Fordwich, returned with his mother to that parish, where, at the age of 32, he served as churchwarden; but in 1637 his son (John) was baptized in the Parish of Sturry,[6] within half a mile of Fordwich.[17] He married Anne ————, who was possibly, as has been suggested, a daughter of the stepfather by a first wife; but it is also possible that when, in 1665, their son John spoke[18] of Mr. Gosmer as his "grandfather," it was not because of his mother's parentage, but because through his father he was a step-grandson.[2]

Thompson, on page 207, named among the settlers who arrived at Southampton, Long Island, during the first twelve months, 1640-41, a "John Gosman" (written "John Gosmer" on page 208) and a "John Woodruff"[19]; while the pages of the Southampton Town Records show that this only one adult John Woodruff of the period in Southampton was a member of the Gosmer household. In addition, this John Woodruff had a son John and daughters Anne and Elizabeth; names of Woodruff-Gosmer parents and grandparents. It is, therefore, only reasonable to presume that it was the John Woodruff born in 1604 who accompanied his mother, Elizabeth, and his stepfather on their

PLATE C

THE SOUTHAMPTON LANDS

THIS Map was made especially for this book from the Government surveys, with additions by Frederick S. Smith, C.E., to show the approximate localities of Gosmer-Woodruff lands; which, sometimes an acre or two, sometimes two or three hundred acres, were widely scattered (for references, see Notes Nos. 27, 30, 32, 34, 40, 49, 53, 54, 61, 62, 69, 70, 71, 73, 78, 81, 83, 84, 85) from West Hampton to Sag Harbor. The properties within the limits of this map that have been identified are roughly indicated by the small crosses (+) placed (in order W. to E. and N. to S.) at or near the following places:

Canoe Place	Southampton Town Lots (3)
Pine Div. of Meadows	Little Plain
Shinnecock Hills	Old Town
Beach Div. of Meadows	Head of Pond
Cold Spring	Water Mill (Mill Neck)
Sebonac	Towd
Ox Pasture	Scuttle Hole Pond
Great Plain	Long Pond
Halsey's Neck	Sagg (Sagaponack)
Captain's Neck	Brushy Neck (Sag Harbor)
First Neck	

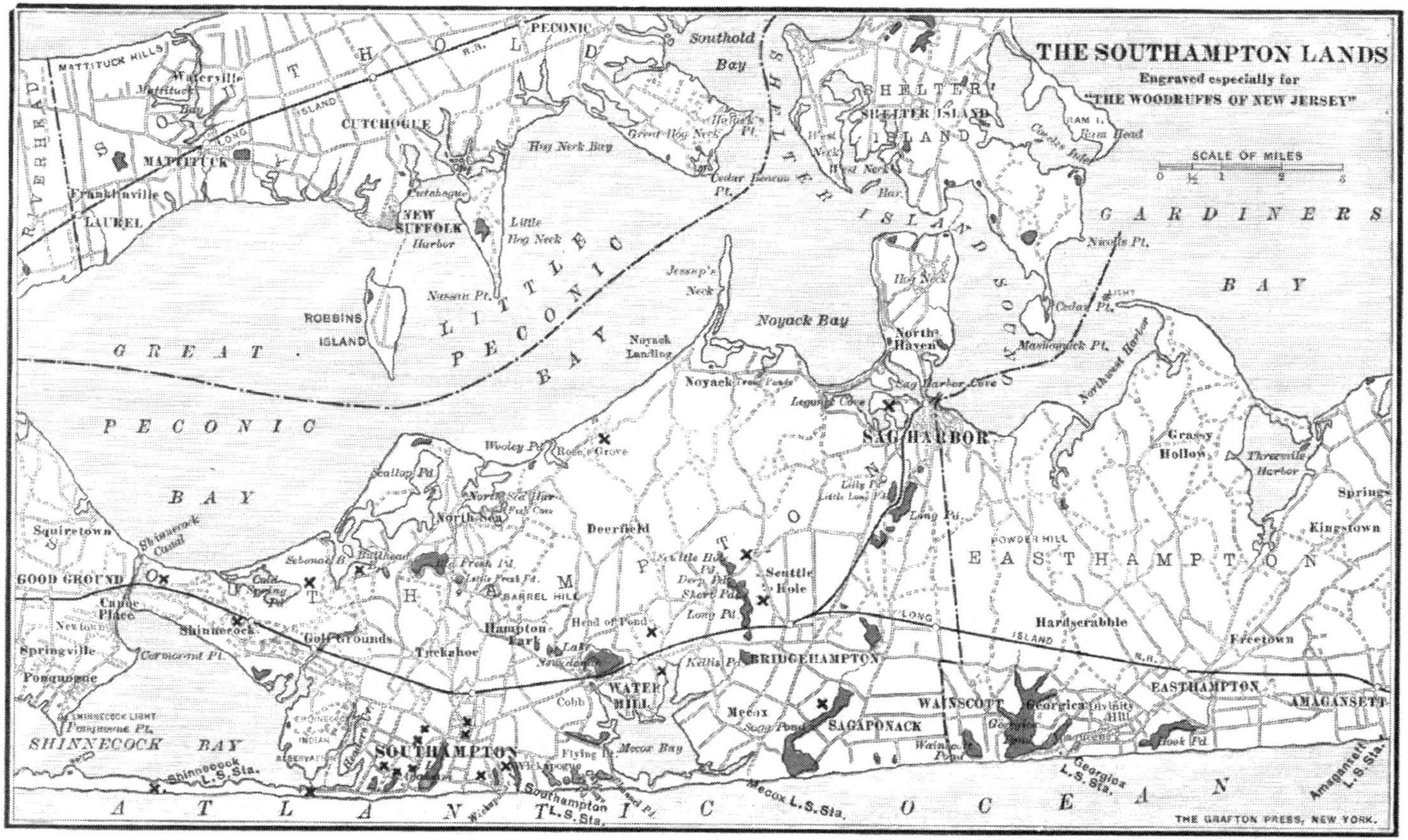

THE SOUTHAMPTON LANDS
Engraved especially for
"THE WOODRUFFS OF NEW JERSEY"
SCALE OF MILES
GARDINERS BAY
GREAT PECONIC BAY
LITTLE PECONIC BAY
SHELTER ISLAND SOUND
SHINNECOCK BAY
ATLANTIC OCEAN
SOUTHOLD
SOUTHAMPTON
EASTHAMPTON
SHELTER ISLAND
RIVERHEAD
MATTITUCK HILLS
Waterville
MATTITUCK
Franklinville
LAUREL
CUTCHOGUE
PECONIC
Southold Bay
NEW SUFFOLK
Robbins Island
Noyack Bay
Noyack
SAG HARBOR
North Haven
Deerfield
BRIDGEHAMPTON
WATER MILL
SAGAPONACK
WAINSCOTT
EASTHAMPTON
AMAGANSETT
Hardscrabble
Freetown
Kingstown
Springs
Grassy Hollow
Tuckahoe
Hampton Park
GOOD GROUND
Canoe Place
Squiretown
Springville
Ponquogue
Shinnecock
Mecox
Cobb
Mecox Bay
Shinnecock L.S. Sta.
Southampton L.S. Sta.
Mecox L.S. Sta.
Georgica L.S. Sta.
Amagansett L.S. Sta.
THE GRAFTON PRESS, NEW YORK.

PLATE C

journey to Lynn and Southampton in 1639-40,[20] and so became the immigrant ancestor of the New Jersey Woodruffs.[20] With him came his wife Anne and the baby John, destined to later become one of the founders of Elizabethtown, New Jersey, so that the baby's descendants enjoy the distinction of having two immigrant ancestors.[21]

For years after the founding of Southampton, although the land was "honorably purchased of its original owners, yet the settlers never saw a moment's rest for fear of their dreaded neighbors. In the field a guard was kept; at night none knew at what hour the alarm would sound; to meeting, on the Lord's day, they went as men prepared for instant war; every male, from 16 years of age to 60, was enrolled in the ranks."[22] Under such circumstances it might be expected that the stepson and his wife would live with their parents, both no longer young,[23] and the belief is confirmed by Mr. Gosmer's statement (in the deed that was his will[61]) that their younger son, John, born in Southampton, whom he adopted, "hath lived with me from a child."[24] In those patriarchal days, even more than now, as a member of Mr. Gosmer's household John Woodruff would not have been considered one of the "heads of families," and, therefore, would not appear in the List of May, 1649.[25] There seems, indeed, to have been no opportunity in the town records until on April 30, 1657 (when he was 53 years of age), he is named among the arms-bearing men to whom gunpowder was served out because of an Indian attack on the town.[26]

On Sept. 17th of the same year Mr. Gosmer "bought an hundred pound lot of John Topping with the housing and fences and all his accommodations, with all the privileges there unto belonging in Southampton,"[27] which he handed over to his stepson; possibly to qualify him as his successor in the whaling squadron, which he became the same year.[28] In that year also (but probably later than the above) John Woodruff is on the list of the representatives of the town houses, while Mr. Gosmer's name is omitted;[29] and he is recorded in the Plan[30] as having, in 1659, succeeded the latter in the Gosmer homestead. In 1659, also, he is for the first time mentioned as exchanging land.[31] On Feb. 20, 1660-61, the 1657 gift of house and land to him was registered by Mr. Gosmer,[32] after which the name of Gosmer disappeared from the records. Apparently, therefore, John Gosmer, who had retired from active work in 1657, died in 1661; and John Woodruff, then 57 years of age, reigned in his stead. In 1661 and 1662 he was only recorded as a successful plaintiff, as on an important jury, as giving in his "ear-mark,"[33] and as dealing in land.[34] In 1663, at the town meeting of May 1st, when new rules were established regarding the keeping up of fences to prevent the trespassing of "cattell, sheepe, goats and hoggs" that had been breeding quarrels and lawsuits, he was elected and "sworne impounder."[35]

In 1664 the times suddenly changed. At its foundation a little republic in itself, Southampton soon entered "into combinacon with the Jurisdiction of Connecticote."[36] The relation continued practically unchanged until on March 12, 1664, Charles II granted Long Island (and other territories) to his brother James, Duke of York; and, against the wish of its people, Suffolk county, with its chief town Southampton, became a part of the Province of New York.[37] In the following year, under the "Duke's Laws," promulgated at the Hempstead convention in March, 1665, Suffolk county was made the "East Riding (court district) of Yorkshire."[38] Townsmen and General Courts (Town Meetings) ceased to exist, and a new tribunal was established called the "Court of the Constable and Overseers." "All the evils anticipated by the people were to be fully realized. All complaints were met in the manner that might be expected from those who considered that they were commissioned by Heaven to rule and that the people were born to obey. Gov. Nicholls was succeeded by Gov. Lovelace, whose character as a ruler may be learned from his remark, that the only way to keep the people quiet was to lay such taxes upon them as should leave no time for thinking of anything else than how to pay them."[39]

Many good men went into opposition, and perhaps John Woodruff was among them. For, excepting such mention in land matters[40] as would be expected for a large proprietor, he does not appear in the records until the final entry of Feb. 22, 1669, when he joined in signing a petition to "our honorable Governor Gen'l Lovelace" that they might not be deprived of "those our privilidges which at great rate wee have procured with much dificulty and danger wee have soe many years possessed."[41] Possibly, also, his absence from public life was, at least in part, due to his having grown older than his years; for he was "weak in Body" when, on May 4, 1670, he made the will[42] that was proved on June 1st. He had died on May 9th, in the 66th year of his age.

In his will he gave unto his "Eldest son John Woodruff of Elizabeth Town, one half crowne piece of money in full of all portions and Patrimony whatsoever, to be expected from mee, or out of any part of my estate"; and to his daughters, Anne[43] and Elizabeth,[44] each £20, to be paid after the widow's death. These small legacies usually indicated that the heirs concerned had already received their portions, on their marriage or their going out into the world, but the peculiar and particular wording in the case of the eldest son may perhaps mean that family friction was not entirely avoided when the younger brother was adopted as son, and made heir, by the step-grandfather.   The testator further made the "wife Anne Woodruff and my youngest son John Woodruff joynt Executors"; and left "all the rest of my Estate both land and chattels and goods and house-hold stuffe to be to ye only proper behoofe and benefitt of my said Execs."   By the Inventory attached to the will we further know that there had already been "one half of ye Land Howsings and Accommodations clearly by Deed of Gift disposed of to his son John"; obviously the younger son.   (Search has failed to find the Deed.)

This Inventory, when compared with others of the place and period, shows that, for his times, John Woodruff was a man of wealth and refinement; and a study of the other too scanty information within reach has given the impression that had he less unselfishly sacrificed himself to the interests of his parents, his family, and his town, the man who was Churchwarden at 32 would have taken up more room in the records.   The little there is, however, is to his honor; and from the requirements of the at that time important and difficult post of "impounder," to which he was elected, it may be inferred that he was upright, of tact and sound judgment, and, generally, of a character and standing that commanded the confidence and respect of all, both high and low, in the community.   Doubtless he, too, like John Gosmer,[45] lies with the other founders of Southampton, in the old South End burying-ground, and his tombstone, also, has crumbled into dust; but, more fortunate than his stepfather, there are ever-increasing generations of direct descendants to keep his name before the eyes of men.

III

THE TWO SONS JOHN

PLATE D.—THE GOSMER-WOODRUFF HOMESTEAD, 1648-1728.

THE TWO SONS JOHN

OF the two sons named John by our ancestor John Woodruff, the Immigrant,[46] the elder was baptized in 1637, in the parish of Sturry,* in Kent, England. He doubtless accompanied his parents and grand-parents[47] on the journey from Fordwich to Southampton, Long Island, in 1639 or 1640, but does not appear in the records of the latter town until April 30, 1657, when he (then twenty years of age) was included in a list of arms-bearing men.[48]

He was first mentioned as a landowner on Feb. 20, 1659-60; and about the same time he married a daughter of Mr. John Ogden, of Southampton. His father-in-law added to his land, and later, in 1664, gave him the "house and home lot" on Main street Mr. Ogden had bought from his nephew (or cousin), John Ogden, on the latter's departure from Southampton.[49] On Jan. 4, 1660-61, "John Woodruff, Jun. his daughter Sarah was borne."[50] He was joint plaintiff with Mr. Ogden in an action of trespass of Sept. 3, 1661, in which the parties came to an agreement. There were dealings in land; and at a town meeting on May 1, 1663, he was elected a "Cunstable."[51] In the burning question of the Topping Purchase he testified, on Feb. 2, 1663-64, that he was present "When Waya-combone delivered unto Mr. John Ogden quite seizen and possession of all ye lands" Mr. Ogden had sold to the town of Southampton, but Captain Topping claimed; the Court decided against the latter.[52]

It was in 1664 that the bitter discontent began because King Charles had granted Long Island (and other territories) to his brother James, Duke of York and Albany.

In addition, after John Woodruff, Sen., died his younger brother would have possession of the homestead that ordinarily would have belonged to himself as head of the family; and it is possible, also, that death in his own household further made longer residence in South-ampton distasteful to the elder son. So it was but natural he should join his father-in-law, Mr. Ogden, in the emigration to New Jersey.

21

Between Aug. 29th and Sept. 7, 1665, he recorded the sales of his house to Robert Woolley, the husband of his sister Anne,[53] and of his land to other fellow townsmen. On the latter date "Sarah Woodruff ye wife of John Woodruff, Jr., of Southampton" confirmed the above sales.[54] How John Woodruff, Jr., could have had a daughter "Sarah," born in 1661, and a wife "Sarah" living on Sept. 7, 1665, and yet on Feb. 7, 1666, or even two or three months earlier, have arrived in Elizabeth Town, as Dr. Hatfield states,[55] with no children and a wife "Mary," evidently needs explanation.[56]

At Elizabethtown, on April 27, 1691, when only fifty-four years old, but "in hazard of life," he made his will,[57] and on May 25th it was proved. His bold signature to the original will at Trenton (Old Essex Wills) is character-revealing! Dr. Hatfield (passim) has told us much, but not enough, of his gallant career as Ensign, High Sheriff, Magistrate, and a leading citizen who stood up bravely against the arbitrary course of the Proprietors. It is earnestly to be hoped that his descendants[58] will tell us the story of his life with the fullness that is so evidently his due.

From the dates there can be no doubt that John Woodruff, Jun., the second son, was born in Southampton, but the year of his birth is unknown;[59] for genealogical purposes, however, it may be put down at about 1650.[60] On July 29, 1659, there is the following record: "Be it known unto all that are present and to come that I, John Gosmer of Southampton upon Long Island in America (Gentleman), have given and granted and by this my present Deed have confirmed to my adopted sone John Woodruf whoe hath lived with me from a child, All my goods and chattells, howses and lands with all the appurtenances, thereunto belonging, and all privileges pertaining thereunto; To have and to hold and to enjoy the above mentioned gifts as his owne forever. Also Elizabeth the wife of ye said John Gosmer (gent.) hath consented and confirmed all the above mentioned gifts in witness whereof they have boath of them hereunto set to their hands and seals this Day of July 29; in the year of ye nativity of our Lord Christ one thousand six hundred fifty-nine."[61] This adopted son was presumably the younger brother.[62]

His first appearance by his own act in the town records was in June, 1666, when he (then probably about sixteen years of age) gave in as his earmark (brand for cattle, etc.) "a half-penny under the left ear."[62] It was perhaps not until 1670, or later, that he married Hannah Newton.[63] In 1675 he joined in the town agreement to set

apart a house and land to "Bee and remain from time to time and
forever to the use of ye ministry of our said towne, as the providence
of God shall hereafter dispose ministers of the word successively unto
us."[64] On Oct. 26, 1682, and on Jan. 8, 1694, he again recorded
his earmark, this time when giving in one for "his son John Woodruff, Jun.," which was to be "two half-pennys under the left ear which
earmark was his grandmother Woodruff's and is by her made over
to the said John Woodruff, Jun."[65] In the same year he was included, for purposes of taxation, in "The Estemate of the Town of
Southampton for the year 1683."[66] He was a subscriber in 1694 for
two of schoolmaster Mr. Mowbrey's "schollers";[67] and in 1696 he
was among the inhabitants of the town assessed for a contribution
to the "defence of the fronteer."[68] From 1673 to 1698 there are
numerous items,[69] besides those already mentioned, regarding the
division, dealing in, and management of land.

By the Lynn agreement of 1639[70] Southampton land was owned
by the Proprietors as tenants in common, until it was, from time to
time, divided by the drawing of lots; the shares being proportioned
to the amount of money each had contributed to the "undertaking."
To provide a convenient unit the town, in 1648, adopted one-fortieth
of £6,000, £150, as a "lot"; to be subdivided into three "fifties."[71]
Shares passed by inheritance, and could be purchased; the undivided
land was called "commonage." As the divisions were made at different times in separate localities, and as in each division each proprietor was entitled' to his share of homestead, meadow, upland,
arable, and wood lands, their holdings were necessarily widely dis-
persed, and there were naturally very many exchanges between individuals to make their farms better suited to their purposes.[72] Hence
it came about that the "swapping of land" seems to have taken the
place of the "swapping of horses" elsewhere; and John Woodruff
evidently did his share.[69]

His share ended when, on Jan. 14, 1701, he "in health of body"
made his will,[73] and on April 1, 1703, it was proved. Between the
death of his father, in 1670, and his own death in 1703, Southampton had passed through many vicissitudes. In July, 1673, New York
was captured by the Dutch. In a manly petition, of Aug. 14th, the
"Inhabitants of the East Riding of Long Island (namely, Southampton, Easthampton, South Hoold, Seataukok, and Huntington)"
surrendered under duress: but, with some aid from Connecticut, and
one "spirited engagement," they successfully resisted the taking of
an oath of allegiance until, on Nov. 10, 1674, Governor Andross

PLATE E

THE DIVISION OF THE EASTERN SECTION OF THE TOWN OF SOUTHAMPTON

(*See Note* 70)

ADAPTED BY FREDERICK S. SMITH, C.E.

N.B.—The figures are in the order of date of division.

1 Great Plain div., 1640-1648.
1A Southampton Old Town div., 1640-1648.
2 Shinnecock Meadows div., 1648.
2A Southampton Town Plot, laid out 1648.
3 North Sea Grant to John Ogden & Co., 1650.
4 Little Plain div., 1651.
5 Seaponack Meadows div., 1653.
5A Sagaponack div., 1653.
6 Mecox div., 1677.
6A Sagaponack div., 1677.
7 Ox Pasture div., 1678.
8 Forty Acre div., 1679.
8A Lot granted John Jessup in (8) div., 1679.
9 Hog Neck div., 1680.
10 Pine div. of Meadows, 1687 and 1737.
11 Shinnecock Hills, leased to Indians, 1703.
11A Shinnecock Neck, leased to Indians, 1703.
12 North Side div., 1712.
12A Thirty Acres div., 1712.
13 Great North div., 1738.
13A Great South div., 1738.
14 Beach Meadows div., 1739.
15 Sag Harbor div., 1745.
16 Twelve Acres div., 1761.
17 Little South div., 1763.
18 Meadows sold by Proprietors, 1846.
19 Shinnecock Hills conveyed by Indians to Proprietors' undivided lands.   By act of 1859.
20 Shinnecock Hills sold by Proprietors, 1860.
20A Shinnecock Neck sold to Indians by Proprietors, 1860.

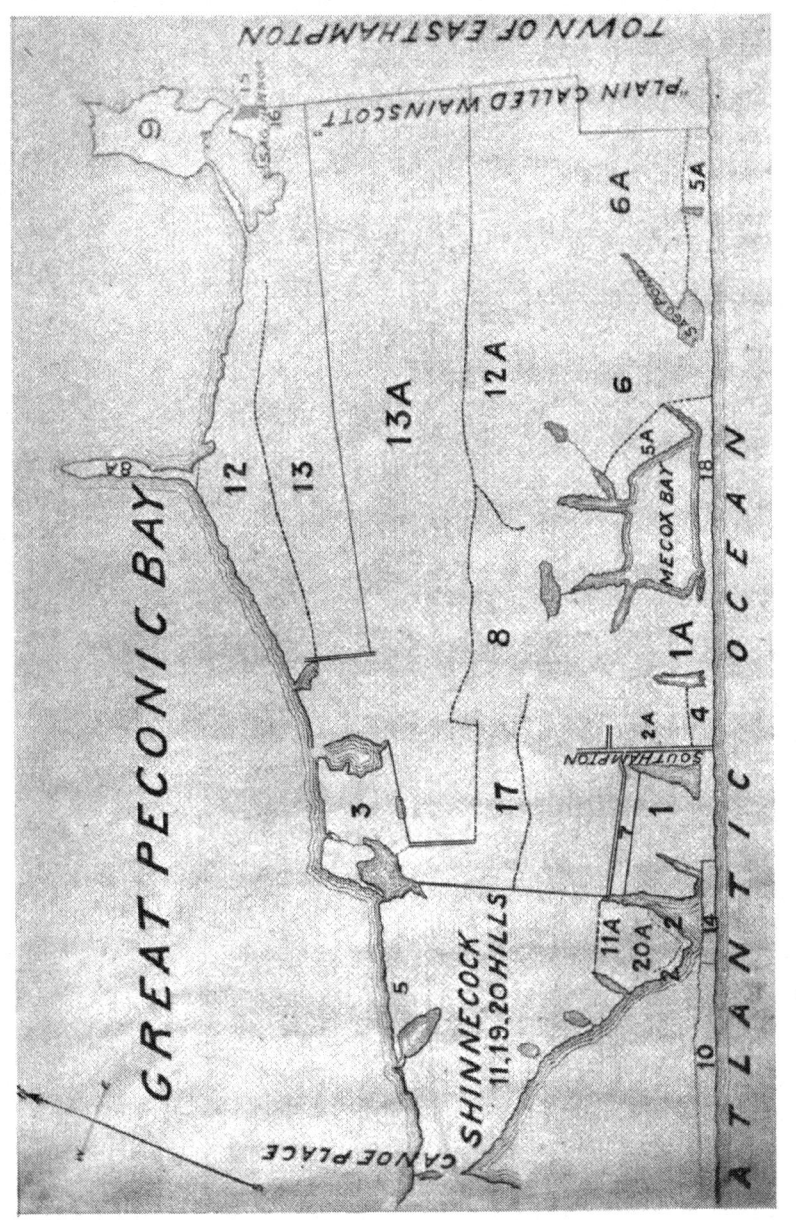

PLATE E.

replaced the Dutch. Instead of rewarding the East Riding for its brave loyalty, the Governor promptly forced the inhabitants to take out, and pay for, new patents for land that was already indisputably their own. The later change of their lord's title from Duke of York to James II only increased the power to oppress, until the revolution of 1686 brought relief.[74]

No doubt John Woodruff did his duty as a good citizen, but the records do not show that he took a prominent part in public affairs. Born with the silver spoon in the mouth that deprives of one incentive to exertion, although soon surpassed in wealth by many in the growing community, yet still the possessor (as his will shows) of broad and scattered acres, now unhappily subjected to grinding taxation and extortion, and with ten children to bring up, he was perhaps one of those upon whom Gov. Lovelace and his successors had laid such taxes as to "leave no time for thinking of anything else than how to pay them";[75] and was what we would, nowadays, call "land poor."

In his will[76] he bequeathed his possessions to his wife Hannah, his sons Samuel, Joseph, Benjamin, Nathaniel, Isaac and Jonathan, and his daughters Sarah (Davis), Hannah, Abigail and Elizabeth, of whom, when his will was drawn, in 1701, all, from Nathaniel down, were not yet twenty-one years old. To his second surviving son, Joseph, who had emigrated to New Jersey,[77] and had, therefore, probably already received a portion in money, he left twenty pounds and a remote reversionary interest in lands willed to the younger brothers. To the daughters he gave ten pounds each on their coming of age, Sarah no doubt having had a portion on her marriage, and the others to be similarly cared for by his heirs. To his wife and his other sons he bequeathed all his houses and lands, including commonage.[78]

The home lot was on the east side of Main street (Southampton), next south of the lot cornering on the "Hampton Road" to Bridge-hampton, Easthampton, etc.,[79] its "three acres" of 1648[80] having been later extended eastward "as much as may be," to be made up for by surrendering land elsewhere.[81] The site of the Gosmer-Woodruff homestead is now occupied by the house of Mr. Josiah Foster. After the original building had, in 1703, come into the hands of John's son, Samuel, it was rebuilt and remodeled to some extent,[82] and as thus altered is shown in Illustration D, in Vol. I, of Southampton Town Records (frontispiece) and in Mr. Howell's History (opposite page 148). On April 12, 1728, Samuel Woodruff and Sarah his wife deeded[83] this property, that had been eighty years in the Gosmer and Woodruff families, to Mr. Francis Pelletreau. The house, which was of some consequence for the time and place, was still standing until within a few years. It was the last in Long Island that retained the old-fashioned rhomboidal window-panes, once in general use, and was for this reason known as the house of the diamond windows.[84]

Samuel Woodruff was on record in Southampton as dealing in land on April 16, 1733, and April 8, 1738,[85] when he was probably sixty-four years of age, and then passed from view. His brothers presumably scattered to the farms that had been bequeathed to them near the town, as there are tombstones of their descendants in the Bridge Hampton (both old and new), Scuttle Hole, and Shelter Island burying-grounds, and perhaps elsewhere; but no graves have been found of John Woodruff's own sons and daughters. Doubtless the tombstones still exist, but possibly are hidden from view beneath the soil.[86] There are occasional records, none indicating residence in Southampton,[87] down to modern times; but few of the blood, and still fewer of the name, of Woodruff, now remain in eastern Long Island. In New Jersey, however, they abound.

NOTE.—Vol. XI, "New York Wills," unrecorded, recently published, shows (p. 27) that Samuel Woodruff, born about 1674—wife Hester—son of John Woodruff, 1650-1703, all of Southampton, L. I., died between 1715 and 1717, leaving a son Samuel. It was doubtless this son Samuel—wife Sarah—who on April 12, 1728, sold the Gosmer-Woodruff homestead and later conveyed lands.

IV

THE WESTFIELD WOODRUFFS

PLATE F

THE WESTFIELD NEIGHBORHOOD

MAP drawn by Mr. O. L. P. Meyer (Elizabeth, N. J.) from Sheet No. 6 of the Topographic Atlas of New Jersey, and an unpublished chart of the 1699-1700 Division prepared by the late Mr. Ernest L. Meyer.

Roselle (on the Map) is just west of Elizabeth, Westfield just east of Plainfield.

In revised edition, Lots 148 and 149, plotted by Prof. S. R. Winans, Map retraced by Mr. Morgan Morris (Morristown, N. J.).

THE WESTFIELD WOODRUFFS

A JOSEPH WOODRUFF (1676-1742) lies buried at Westfield, New Jersey, whose existence in his own right has not been recognized by modern historians. These have merged the scanty records of his life into that of his Elizabeth Town cousin, Joseph (1674-1746), or sometimes into that cousin's son, Joseph; but their error has been the more excusable because the cousins were only two years apart in date of birth, and because not only they, but their fathers and grandfather, all bore the same given names as well as surname. The Etown father, John Woodruff (1637-91), was the elder son of the Immigrant, John Woodruff (1604-70), while the Westfield Joseph's father was the younger son and brother, John Woodruff (1650-1703), of Southampton, Long Island; from which town our Joseph emigrated to New Jersey.[88]

His Westfield tombstone tells us that he departed this life Feb. 2d, Anno Domini 1741-2, in the sixty-fifth year of his age; so he was born in 1676 or 1677. While living at Southampton, and some seventeen or eighteen years old, he was quite possibly one of the two "schollers" for whom, in 1694, his father subscribed "att twelve shillings In cash per scholler for the Terme of Six Months," they to be taught "In the hours following viz, from Eight to Eleven a Clocke In the forenoone, and from one to five of the clocke In ye afternoone";[89] but nothing is certainly known, excepting that he was included as the second son of John Woodruff in the 1698 list of the inhabitants of Southampton, and that his father's will, signed on the "14 day of January Anno Dom 1700 alias 1701," treated him as one who had already gone from home. There were good reasons why the second son should have sought a career elsewhere. His father, although a wealthy landowner, was, because of extortionate taxation, land poor, and there were five brothers and four sisters to be provided for; while there were influential relatives in New Jersey, where, in 1699, there was to be a distribution of rich lands; and his cousin, Robert Woolley, of Southampton, was also to become an Etown Associate, and draw a Westfield lot.[90] So Joseph transferred the history of our line from Long Island to New Jersey.

Because in 1664 the shifty Duke of York conveyed the territory now known as New Jersey to Lord Berkeley and Sir George Carteret, while his oversea agent, Gov. Nicholls, was, under the Duke's authority, confirming the Indian deeds of the Etown Associates, there came the century of contest between the "Proprietors" of East Jersey (as successors of Carteret) and the "Associates"; in which all on both sides could feel they had been wronged. For many years neither side thrust home, but in 1693 the Proprietors, in the name of James Fullerton, brought an action of Trespass and Ejectment against one Jeffry Jones because of his refusal to take out a patent from them for his lands (his, under Nicholl's grant) and to pay them "Quit Rents." Judgment (on a "special" verdict by the Court) having been rendered against him (and against the "general" verdict of the jury) he appealed to King William in Council, by whom, on Feb. 25, 1696-97, the judgment was set aside, and so Gov. Nicholl's grant confirmed.[91]

Encouraged in this and other ways, the Associates decided to distribute hitherto undivided lands, and by March, 1700, the task had been completed. The pioneers found their way (Ill. F) by blazed trails across Crane's ford (now Cranford) to Westfield,[92] which was long the extreme border of civilization. For the region that now, in many parts, has almost the "finish" of the old countries, was then a wilderness, that in 1665 had sold ten acres for a penny, with a soil generally of stiff clay or gravelly loam for the wooden plows and harrows to grapple with, and with much heavy timber to clear away. Wolves compelled a bounty of thirty shillings, and there were battles to be fought with the Indians, who only ceased to trouble when, in the middle of the century, the French war drew them away, never to return in considerable numbers. So, like other colonists, the settlers long took their muskets to church with them.[93] The "homestead plantation," the 100-acre lot No. 149,[94] of which Joseph Woodruff took possession in 1701, lay "a Cros Raway River," at a great bend, over a mile downstream from Cranford, and some three miles southeast of the modern town of Westfield. To-day, looking at the amphitheater from the old Raritan Road that leads through the bend, southwesterly, or from the new north-and-south Walnut Avenue that crosses the old road, one sees broad, almost level fields of green—with here and there hedgerows, and orchards, and farmhouses half hidden in their shade trees—sloping gently toward the dark background of woods that fringes and marks the semi-circular course of the river. At the southwest the tall smokestacks of the American Felt Mills show over the woods against the sky. Even now a pastoral scene very pleasant to the eye, in its wilder beauty it must have been a home to love that, by 1714, Joseph had wrested from the wilderness for his wife Hannah and their growing family.

In Joseph's will the eldest son named (John) was not born until 1704, but in the beginning of the settlement deaths may have left no record. Certainly, because in 1700 Joseph would have been some twenty-four years of age, and his wife Hannah perhaps seventeen, it would be expected that they came together to New Jersey; and there was an abundant choice at Southampton of maidens of her given name.[95] Practically, however, nothing is known about the wife and mother, excepting that there were ten sons and three daughters to mourn when, but a few months after her comrade's death, she followed to a grave beside him.

> Hannah ye Wife of
> Joseph Woodruff
> Died August the 14th
> Anno Domini 1742
> In ye 58th Year of her
> Age.

Their married life had been one long anxiety. Barely had they safely passed the hardships and dangers of the first days of the new settlement when they were plunged into the forefront of the battle between the Proprietors and Associates, defending their home in the historic Vaughan Ejectment Suit.

In 1686 James Emott received from the Proprietors a patent for 100 acres each of arable, pasture and wood land (Lot 25). It was claimed that at the time he had work done on the land, but no record has been found that between the 1699-1700 division and his death, in April, 1713, he ever disputed Joseph's undisturbed possession of the home his labor was carving out of the wilderness. James Emott left his claim to his widow, a stepdaughter of Gov. Carteret and later of Col. Townley. The widow, on July 1, 1714, was married to the Rev. Edward Vaughan; and in that year's November term of the Supreme Court the husband brought the action of ejectment. Extracts from the Etown Bill in Chancery (page 46) of

1745 and the Answer (page 122) of the Associates state the two sides of the question with sufficient clearness.

THE PROPRIETORS. "And your Orators do further show unto "your Excellency (the Governor) That in the Supreme Court of "New Jersey in the Term of November in the first Year of King "George the First (1714) an Action of Ejectment was brought "on the demise of Edward Vaughan, as Assignee of James Emott, "for recovery of the possession of that 300 acres of land which "had been granted by the Proprietors to James Emott, by Patent, "dated the 6th day of April, 1686, * * *; and of which tract "(elsewhere, of a part of which tract) one Joseph Woodruff had "possessed himself under colour of the Clinker Lot Right (1699- "1700 division) aforesaid; which came to trial in the Terme of "May in the second year of King George the First (1715) and "therein a special verdict was found setting forth the Title of the "Proprietors of East Jersey on the part of the Plaintiff, and the "said Indian purchase by (the Associates) Bailey and others, and "Nicholl's Grant, on the part of the Defendant; which special "verdict was for sundry terms argued by Council learned in the "law on both sides, and afterwards upon mature deliberation "thereon had, the said Supreme Court gave judgment for the "Plaintiff, to wit, in the term of May in the fourth year of King "George the First (1718); which judgement still remains in Force "unreversed, tho' a Writ of Error was brought thereon before the "Governor and Council."

THE ASSOCIATES. "In particular that when Joseph Woodruff, "one of Your Majesty's petitioners' ancestors,[90] by Writ of Error, "brought his Cause before the Governor and Council of this Prov- "ince in the fourth year of Your Majesty's late Royal Father "(1718), in order to obtain a Judgment thence and from thence, "if Judgment were given against him, he intended to have appealed "to his said Majesty then King of Great Britain * * * in "Council, the said Governor and Council would never be prevailed "upon to give a Judgment in the said Cause, but after ten or twelve "years delay and a vast Expense in the Cause, the said Cause dropt "without being decided."

It is evident that in face of King William's adverse decision in 1697,[91] and of Joseph's stern determination to appeal to England rather than submit to injustice, there was a grave dilemma confronting the Governor and Council. Should they decide for Joseph it would be a fatal blow to the entire claim of the Proprietors; if they decided against him it could only stave off that evil a little time and then bring from England both the fatal blow and humiliation for themselves of a second adverse decision. So they naturally welcomed delay.

In 1719 they ordered a transcript of the Supreme Court record, and the filing of errors by the defendant. Two years later more time was granted to the defendant. After another two years, on the motion of the defendant, the transcript was returned to the Supreme Court, "to be examined and amended." Still another twelvemonth, and the amended record was "brought up" by Chief Justice Trent;[97] but the defendant consented to one more year's postponement. At last, in 1725, a "re-hearing in this Cause" was ordered, and on August 19th the "Cause" made its final appearance before the Governor and Council; but after all the long delay, with only this meager and inconclusive outcome:

"Councill was re-heard on both sides in this Cause."

"Curia advisare vult."

And the Court kept on deliberating to the end, if it could be called an end that was never finished.[98] Already, in 1720, to guard against renewed attacks by the Proprietors, the Associates had appointed a Committee of Seven.[99] After 1725 there was further litigation by the Proprietors. The Associates sold lands to provide funds for defense. They petitioned the King. The above quoted Bill in Chancery and its Answer followed. Then came the Revolution, and the issue dropped out of sight. "Such was the end of this "famous struggle, continued for a whole century, and resulting in "the vindication of the original purchasers of the soil, and the defeat "of their opponents."[100]

For Joseph and Hannah, however, the sword of uncertainty hung suspended until their deaths. It was on Jan. 15, 1742, that "Joseph Woodruff, Jr., of the Burrough of Elizabeth,"[101] "Being sickly and weakly in Body," made his will;[102] and on Feb. 2d he died. His executors were his wife Hannah, friend William Miller[103] and son Thomas. To his "Dearly Beloved Wife" he bequeathed the "Best Room in my now (or 'new,' text obscure) Dwelling House";[94] one-third of the "Improvement" (apparently, income, usufruct) of all his lands; one-third of his "Moveable Estate" (personal property), and any overplus of the latter after all charges had been met. To

the heirs who had already received their portions, viz., John, Jonathan, William, Samuel, and Abigail (wife of John Gold), he gave
five shillings each, to be paid out of his "Moveable Estate." Between
Thomas and Hezekiah he divided "all my Homestead plantation
which I now live on Situate, Lying and Being adjoyning to the west
side of the Rahaway River," and "Two pieices or parcels of Salt
Marsh or Meadow Lying and being at the bottom of Tremby's
Neck."[104] To Joseph he gave the "House and Land" bought from
Daniel Talmage, Dec. 11, 1741. To Nathaniel he gave the "House
and Plantation bought of Joseph Bird, lately deceased." To Isaac
he gave "my piece of Salt Meadow Lying and Being by Murthes
Creek";[105] and Nathaniel was to pay him thirty pounds. To Benjamin he gave "my Negro Boy named Lewey"; and forty pounds to
be paid him (by Thomas and Hezekiah) when "he shall arrive at the
age of 16 years old." To each of his daughters Sarah and Joanna
Woodruff he gave sixteen pounds. Surely, he had well provided for
his goodly family! Forced from his boyhood's home by extortionate
taxation, into a struggle with the hardships and dangers of a wilderness, then to be harassed by the long, anxious contest in defense of
his lands, that he so overcame the obstacles to success and died more
than ordinarily prosperous for his day plainly shows that Jonathan's[106] "honored father Joseph" was a brave, strong man.[107]

Hezekiah Woodruff was worse off in the matter of records even
than his father, Joseph. At the time of his birth, in 1724, Westfield
had begun to have a community life of its own apart from Elizabeth,
yet has left no annals of that period. A good authority has stated
that a young man who had sinned burned the earlier church records
to destroy the minutes of his trial and conviction; and at least,
although the church was organized in 1727 its records date back only
to 1759, while the town records do not begin until 1794, when Westfield was set off as a township. Up to 1759, therefore, our chief
sources of local information are wills and tombstones.

From the latter we learn that Hezekiah died Oct. 22, 1776, in
his 52d year; and Mary, his wife, on July 21, 1772, in the 44th
year of her age. In his will (T.—20:37), dated Oct. 25, 1776,[108]
Hezekiah named as an executor his "Loving Father John Stites"
(1706-1782); whose will (T. 23:436, dated Feb. 13, 1781) named
as daughter "Mary Woodruff, deceased"; while the will (T. 35:512,
dated June 28, 1796) of John's son, Dr. Hezekiah Stites, named
as nephew, Dr. Hezekiah Stites Woodruff (1754-1842), who was

one of the sons of Hezekiah and Mary Woodruff. As Hezekiah Woodruff's own father was unquestionably Joseph Woodruff; as his mother died too soon after his father's death to have given him a stepfather, and as in early records "father" often stood for "father-in-law,"[2] there can be no doubt that, in accordance with our family traditions, Hezekiah's wife Mary was a daughter of John Stites.

The Hon. John Stites, ancestor of many honored citizens of New Jersey, was born at Hempstead, Long Island, in 1706, and died at Springfield, New Jersey, April 21, 1782. He was a Chosen Freeholder and Justice of Etown, and a Deputy in the Provincial Congress of New Jersey in 1775.[109] As his tombstone at Springfield tells us, he "lived beloved and died lamented by Church and State."

Excepting the record of the membership of Hezekiah and his wife Mary in the Scotch Plains Baptist Church,[109] her father having been a prominent Baptist, no other trace has been found of their lives up to the date of his will in October,·1776. Crippled by the death of the wife in July, 1772, at least at the end "Sick and weak of body," and dying at the very beginning of the Revolutionary War, he may not have been able to do more than sympathize with the known ardent patriotism of his brothers and his sons; but it is quite as likely that our ignorance of his share is due to lack of records. From what is known of his circumstances it is certain that he was well born, well married, well off, and a respected citizen; to judge from his sons, he may have been very much more.

In his will, after a special gift of a team of horses, a yoke of oxen, etc., to his son Richard, he bequeathed his property in trust to his executors, John Stites and Abner Corey, for the support, until sold, of his family; the net proceeds to then be "put at intrust" for five years for the same purpose. At the end of the period Hezekiah Stites Woodruff (provided for by his uncle, Hezekiah Stites, see Sketch V) was to receive £50, Hannah (Winants) £5, the two children of Abigail (Pack, Paiks or Parks—records obscure) £5 equally divided, Margaret, Mary and Sarah £30 each. The "remainding. part" of his estate was to be equally divided between his five sons, Stites, Richard, Hiram, Benjamin and John.[110] This provision of a "trust" not being customary in that day, was possibly made expedient by the Revolution's disturbance of existing conditions.

It may have been from the same cause that in 1784 the son Stites sold the "homestead plantation"[94] and so severed us descendants of Dr. Hezekiah Stites Woodruff from our first New Jersey home, near which, however, many cousins still well maintain the family name.

In the later deeds conveying our ancestors' lands a boundary mark quite often named is "Tooker's (Tucker) lane," which (now closed) used to be the way from the Raritan Road (Ill. F), near where it is crossed by the modern Walnut Avenue, to the late John Tucker's attractive old residence (occupied in 1902 by Mr. Joseph Holland) on the banks of the Rahway. This is said to have been built as a home and school by Jean and Marie de Vermont Touchembert, formerly of the Island of Guadaloupe, who, in 1794, bought the land from Jacob Winans, who had, in 1784, bought it from Stites Woodruff.[94] A short distance to the eastward of this house (see mark in No. 148, Ill., F), on the land of Mr. and Mrs. Marx Riefel,[94] there are still traces of the foundations (and well) of a good-sized dwelling-house, that from a knoll looked over the high bank with its fringe of trees, across the river to the wooded shore beyond. After John Tucker bought the property from the Touchemberts, in 1802, this older building was no longer used as a dwelling, but it was still standing in the lifetime of the present neighbors: a house built of stone for the ground story and above of oak. From the situation and the circumstances there need be no doubt that it was the home of our ancestor Hezekiah (died 1776), even if not the "now Dwelling House" of his father, Joseph (died 1742); so is an additional inducement to their descendants to visit the old "homestead plantation."

V

DR. HEZEKIAH STITES WOODRUFF

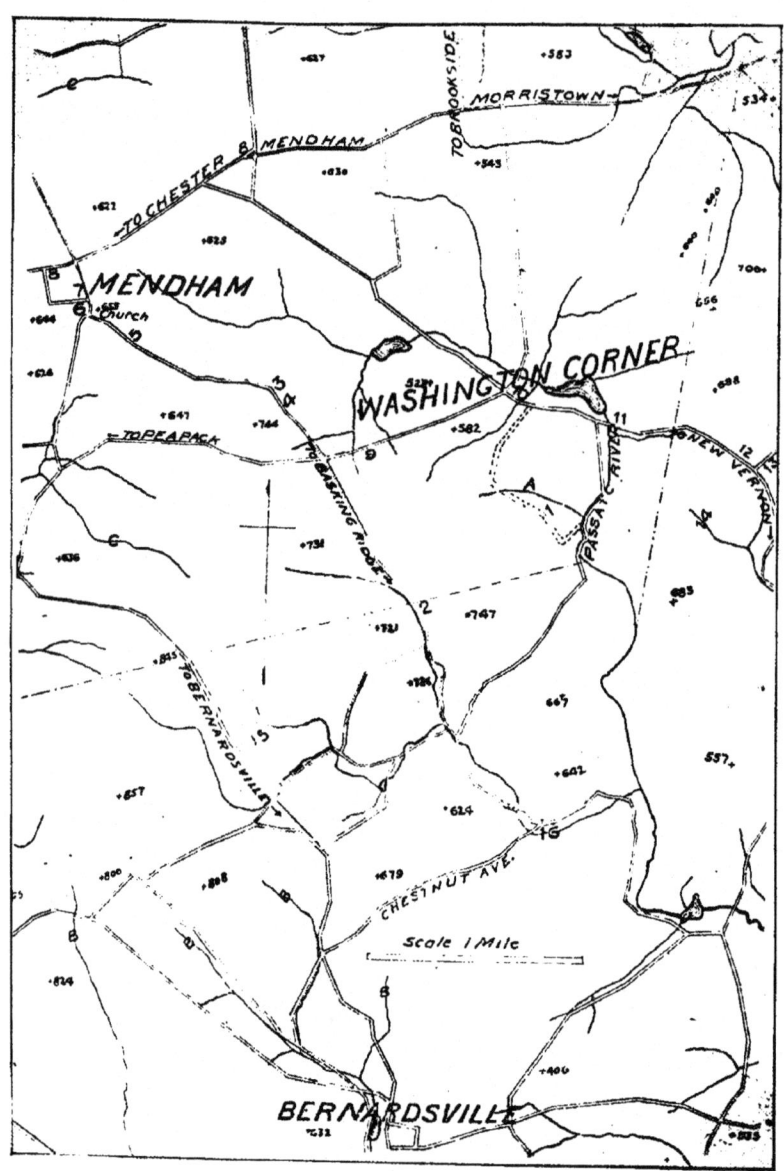

PLATE G.

PLATE G

WASHINGTON CORNER AND MENDHAM

THIS Map has been reduced and adapted, from New Jersey Geological Survey sun-prints (three inches per mile), by Frederick S. Smith, C.E., of Morristown, N. J. Figures 000 denote altitude of heights. Such of Nos. 1 to 16, below, as refer to homes, indicate sites of dwelling-houses concerned, e. g. the property No. 1 extends easterly to Brook A, westerly touches boundary of Property No. 2. The dotted lines beside No. 1 show course of private road through farms and woods. Several of the dates are approximate only.

A, Mine Run, B, Mine Brook, Note 118; C, Streams flowing into Raritan River.

1. Dr. H. S. Woodruff, 1776-1782, Note 118. 2. Dr. H. S. Woodruff, 1776-1827, Note 118. 3. Dr. Ebenezer Blachly, Note 140. 4. Dr. H. S. Woodruff, 1792-1810, Note 139 and text. 5. Dr. Absalom Woodruff, 1835-6, Note to App. B. 6. Dr. H. S. Woodruff, 1810-1828, Note 142 and text. 7. Dr. Absalom Woodruff, 1836-1843, Note to App. B. 8. Dr. H. S. Woodruff, 1828-1830-4, Note 142 and text. 9. Dr. H. S. Woodruff, Notes 118, 139, 140. 10. Preserve Riggs, Note to App. B.; 118. 11. Dr. William Leddell, Note 118; App. E. 12. Capt. Henry Wick, Note 118; App. D. 13. Capt. Bettin's grave, Note 128. 14. Camp, N. J. Brigade, Note 126 and text. 15. Somerset Inn, a modern landmark. 16. Logtown, Note 118, at end.

DR. HEZEKIAH STITES WOODRUFF

HEZEKIAH STITES WOODRUFF, better remembered as "Stites Woodruff," was born on the 28th of June, 1754, presumably at Westfield, N. J., where his parents, Hezekiah and Mary (Stites) Woodruff, were then living.[111] As has been told, his family was of standing in the community, but because no local annals of the period remain,[112] all we know of his youth is the family tradition[113] that he was brought up by his mother's childless brother, Hezekiah Stites, of Cranbury, in the County of Middlesex, "practitioner of Surgery and Physick," as he styled himself in his will.[114] This will sustains the tradition in that (while leaving some Long Island lands to his nephew, John Stites, Jr., and dividing many of his personal belongings by name among those near to him) his chief heir was his namesake, to whom he bequeathed his "Bonds, Mortgages, Bills, Notes and Book Debts" and "all and every other thing not heretofore given of Household Goods, Plate, &c.,"[115] besides making him co-executor with the brother and uncle John Stites and their connection, Jonathan Hampton.[116]

Whether or not the uncle hoped for a successor to his own practice, from the fact that the nephew became the first of the multitude of physicians in our family, it is hardly possible that he did not learn something of his profession while still at Cranbury. It may, therefore, have been only to "finish" that our great-grandfather later became a pupil of the widely known Dr. Ebenezer Blachly, 1735-1805, of Mendham, N. J., and, to make the story complete, fell in love with the doctor's eldest daughter.[117] It followed that Hezekiah Stites Woodruff, M.D., aged 22, and Mary Blachly, aged 17, were married on May 11th of the eventful year 1776, and settled beside her parents and relatives (Ill. G, 1, 3, 11, 12).

Their new home was near Washington Corner, in Mendham Township, Morris County,[118], their lands extending over the border into Bernard Township, Somerset County (of which latter the doctor sometimes called himself). The house, still standing (but with an added modern wing), was a two-storied building, creditable for its day, near by one of the springs of the little Mine Run, that, starting from other springs higher up the foothill, swiftly takes its mile-long course down the side, through the woods, into the Passaic. Tradition doubtless truly tells of a well-kept establishment, with a few slaves, and a certain stateliness in keeping with the position and prospects of the young couple; but their life in this pleasant home quickly ceased to be all joy. In October (1776) grief came with the death of the father, Hezekiah Woodruff,[119] and in December the war that had been waged for a twelvemonth drew near their doorstep when General Lee was captured at Basking Ridge (a mile from Bernardsville, Ill. G), and Washington's victories at Trenton and Princeton began the movement that led our wearied soldiers to Morristown and the Lowantica Valley, but a few miles away. That winter a scourge of smallpox and other dread diseases in the camp gave urgent need for the aid of every physician within call.

With all of both their families ardent patriots, there can be no doubt of their anxious interest in the struggle, even if we cannot verify the tradition that just after marriage he tore himself away from her to give his medical services to his country. The records have also failed to support the more general family belief that he was a regularly appointed surgeon in the army; but there is unquestioned evidence that he was so regarded by his contemporaries, and that he dressed the wounds of many of our soldiers.[113][120] At most, though, his service could not have been continuous, because he also maintained an extensive practice for miles around his home, and was retained with an annual fee (probably at that time not unusual) as the physician of some of the wealthy families in the neighborhood; and that he was at home when our army was quartered at Morristown is indicated by the fact that Gen. Washington, and doubtless other officers, are known to have sometimes spent the night at his house, which, from its situation (Ill. G, 1, 14), would, in 1780, have been a convenient resting place.[118] Knowing these things, and knowing that, admirable as is the work already done, returns from many (Heitman says one-tenth) of the organizations have not yet been found, there seems hope that further research may some day bring to light his official record, even if only as a Volunteer Surgeon in the parts of the army twice wintering here.[121]

The smallpox winter, during which the doctor, no doubt, did his duty, at last passed. Then the British, when withdrawing from New Jersey to attack Philadelphia by sea, troubled his childhood's home. On June 26, 1777, they advanced in force from Perth Amboy through Woodbridge (Map in Sketch IV) to Westfield and Scotch Plains (Fanwood), where there was a sharp engagement; so must have passed near the old Woodruff "homestead plantation" on the bank of the Rahway. Their attack happily failed, but that day our doctor's brother Stites[119] was made poorer by "32 Good Sheep" and "1 Large four year Bull."[110] [122] There was good fortune for themselves, though, when, on Sept. 22d, the first born[123] came; but their happiness must have been dimmed by the disheartening news from Brandywine and Germantown.

Then followed for our army the winter of peril and suffering at Valley Forge: cold, starvation, putrid fever, death. "That patriotism which rises and expends itself in sudden ebullition is of ordinary growth—-is a fever contagious in crowds—whilst that which endures under the deprivation of food and raiment, amid the severities of winter and the perils of disease and battle, is as rare as it is estimable; but it is not so rare as that which, in the noncombatant, withstands the forcible, hourly, hopeless, unremunerated drain of the purse. Against the exactions therefore of the army even the friendly farmer . . . opposed the resources of his cunning; and though he did not furnish supplies to the enemy, who tempted him with gold, he concealed them from his friends who could pay for them, at best, in almost worthless paper, and frequently only in naked promises. . . . General Washington could obtain relief only by the strenuous exertions of his best officers."[124] To their efforts, however, he added his personal appeal, and wrote to our doctor (as doubtless to many others), "For God's sake send me some cattle, my men are starving." Mortgaging property to provide the ready money needed to buy the cattle, our great-grandfather himself convoyed them on the long march from his home; when not met, as had been arranged, beyond the British lines, evaded their pickets, brought the cattle safely into camp, and was publicly thanked by General Washington.[125]

After the engagement at Monmouth, in June, 1778, excepting for the border warfare with the Staten Island refugees our State had a comparative rest until, toward the end of 1779, the army a second time went into winter quarters at Morristown. From the town[126] the encampment extended westerly along the Jockey Hollow Road (Western Avenue) past the Wick house, over the crossroad, to where the New Jersey Brigade lay within a mile or so of the doctor's home (Ill. G, 12, 14, 1).[113] [118] The winter was exceptionally severe, the district was drained almost to exhaustion of supplies, our soldiers

PLATE H

SOME OF THE WOODRUFF HOMES

I. WICK HOUSE, at Washington Corner, N. J. (Ill. G, 12), home of our ancestor. Henry Wick (App. D), was so called when log dwellings were in fashion. It was built between 1746 and 1775, probably nearer the former year, but the exact date has not been ascertained.

II. THE HILL TOP CHURCH, Mendham, N. J. (Ill. G). The foreground shows a part of the homestead land of our great-grandfather, Dr. H. S. Woodruff (Ill. G, 6; Note 142), from 1810 to 1828. The rank growth covers the ruined foundations of the Ezra Fairchild School Building (Note 147).

The church here shown, built in 1860, is the fourth on the same site. The first, erected in 1745, was damaged by lightning in 1813, and in 1816 was replaced by a better one; that was destroyed by fire in 1835, as was its successor also, in 1859.

III. THE MENDHAM HOME (Ill. G, 7), from 1836 to 1843, of our grandfather, Dr. Absalom Woodruff (Ill. I; App. B and Note), is not shown just as it was in his day, in that the piazza (in place of a porch) and the bow-window are presumably, and the rear extension is certainly, modern. Miss Leddell (Note 140) tells us that it was built by a Mr. Axtell; was bought in 1803-4, and long lived in, by Dr. John W. Leddell, and was by him sold to Dr. Woodruff.

It may here be stated that the middle section of the Morristown home (No. 55 South Street) of the latter's son, and our father, Dr. E. B. Woodruff (App. B and Note), built before the Revolution, probably by Sheriff Kinney, in 1775, still stands, but is so masked by its modern wings that a photograph of it would be misleading; and also that, unfortunately, there is no portrait extant of Dr. E. B. Woodruff that does him anything like justice.

IV. PRESENT HOME, Glen Ridge, N. J., of XII; 39-16.

V. PRESENT HOME, Morristown, N. J., of XII; 42-16.

PLATE H.

suffered terribly, and our doctor was again in urgent demand, of which traces might be found by search through the army records of that date at Washington. The ice blockade on New York Bay also caused the border warfare to flourish, so that his old Westfield home, and his brothers there, were in constant danger; but later, when, in June, 1780, there were two attacks in force on Connecticut Farms (Union) and Springfield, our militiamen greatly distinguishing themselves in the repulse, Westfield and the "home plantation" were, fortunately, out of the line of fire, and so escaped damage.[119] [122] [127] On Jan. 1, 1781, there came the mutiny in General Wayne's command, so near the Washington Corner home that the sound of the shots that killed Captain Bettin must have reached the ears of its inmates (Ill. G, 13, 1).[128] In October came the surrender at Yorktown, and then, but for lessened border warfare, New Jersey was little disturbed, until in 1783 there was peace.

Whether because the shock of the mutiny so near the attractive but forest-surrounded home had made village life seem preferable, or from whatever cause, in 1782[129] Dr. Woodruff removed his household to Hopewell Township, Hunterdon County, and settled at Pennington, possibly known to him through his journey to Valley Forge.[125] His home was on the main street, and he held, besides, other village and farm lands.[129] In 1784 he had the pleasure of being made a member of the Medical Society of New Jersey (Wickes),[130] but money troubles were coming to him. A lawsuit[118] [136] delaying payment for his former Mine Run home, from which he had expected ready money, he in turn failed to pay a debt on his new farm lands; so in March, 1784, had to surrender them.[131] [2] [3] [4] As he owned lands in at least two localities, and had an income from his practice, he was still, no doubt, a man of means; but equally, no doubt, he, like his neighbors, had lost heavily by the war.

South Carolina excepted, New Jersey had suffered more than any other State from the drain on the resources of her citizens.[135] The evil results of the rapid depreciation of the paper issues also bore heavily on those who had lent money or supplied services; they received less value than they had given or been promised. As the gradual return to the specie standard brought appreciation, the debtors in turn felt the pinch; but the creditors again suffered through not being paid at all. Of the doctor's fifteen Supreme Court suits,[136] friendly and unfriendly, scattered between 1778 and 1819, some, at least, were plainly to determine a fair equivalent value in fluctuating currency. No doubt very many more disputes were settled in the local courts, and many debts were hopeless of collection. Temporarily, rich had become poor and the poor more poor.

At Pennington, as at Mine Run, he did not stay long enough to leave more than a faint mark, and all the County History has to say of him[137] is, "Among the early physicians was Dr. Woodruff, who practiced some years." The deed[138] conveying his homestead to his successor, Dr. Blachly, is dated Sept. 29, 1792, which, no doubt, approximately indicates the time of the removal of our great-grandparents to a third home; again beside her parents at Mendham, and apparently to fill a family need. The eldest daughter could best care for the mother, who, in grief from the recent death of a son, and herself to die Sept. 18, 1796, may have already needed support; the doctor was to lighten the burden of the father, then 57 years old, and to succeed him in his practice.[139]

As there is no record of their having acquired property on their arrival, they perhaps lived on previously owned property,[118] or with their parents, or in one of the "two other dwelling houses" at the Blachly homestead (Ill. G, 9, 3, 4).[140] Although this had been advertised for sale as early as Nov. 1, 1798, some two years after the mother's death, and the father had died April 19, 1805, it was not until May 10, 1810, that it was sold,[141] and our great-grandparents, on May 18th, found their fourth home on Mendham Hill Top (Ill. G, 6). Northward, the village closed the view; easterly, diagonally across the broad street, were the church and graveyard; looking southerly, over the rounded hillocks of the green valley, they saw Mine Mountain and the other Somerset hills that have made Bernardsville, some four or five miles away, a favored resort. The house, in which the doctor made the longest stay of his busy life, has disappeared, but the boundaries remain unchanged.[142]

During the twenty years from 1810 to 1830 our country, while still to suffer from war, and industrial, monetary, political and other troubles, yet advanced toward the coming prosperity. The doctor was already fifty-six years of age, his wife Mary fifty-one; of their five surviving children, the eldest was thirty-three, the youngest only ten. He had succeeded to his father-in-law's extensive practice; their means had been replenished through inheritance; and for many years their lives were happy. Excepting in the matter of real estate, and the like, the scanty records show few details; but among them it may be noted that as the senior veterans of the Revolution passed away the juniors in turn became the seniors, so in 1824 and 1825, at least, he was chairman (with Lieutenant Reed, secretary) at the meetings of the patriotic citizens of Mendham to arrange for the Fourth of July celebration.[143] Tradition further tells us that he was a man of mark in the community, respected for his high character, and beloved for his helpfulness and kindly humor. His solemnly upbraiding a friend and neighbor, who was having a sleigh painted red and black, for putting it in mourning for the devil, is perhaps typical of the latter; because all his jokes known to us were like this, just good-natured fun, without a hint of malice. Probably his own strong personality has helped to keep them alive, for "as old Dr. Woodruff used to say"[144] is still heard in the land.

Grief, and the beginning of the end, came with the death of the wife of his youth.[145] In 1826 he married Elizabeth, widow of Jacob Dufford.[146] On May 12, 1828, he conveyed his Hill Top homestead to Ezra Fairchild for his widely known school,[147] and probably for a time lived in his Main Street house (Ill. G, 8).[148] He was now, however, well over seventy, and needed rest; so he soon had to give up the Mendham he had loved from his early married days, in 1776, and where he had been beloved. "He was rough and ready in wit and ways, and is affectionately remembered, as all original, natural characters are apt to be."[149]

The last of his many homes was at Succasunna, not far away, where, and at the contiguous Drakesville (now Ledgewood), his sons, Ebenezer and Absalom, were in partnership as the practicing physicians. The latter, in 1835, went to Mendham (App. B, Note), and it rested with his eldest son to care for him. Although probably with too little of his fortune left,[150] from the kindly words of his old neighbors we know that with wife and children and grandchildren around him, and the many new friends he had quickly won, he remained cheery to the end, which came, as the tombstone there records, on Aug. 16, 1842, in the eighty-ninth year of his age. Impulsive, warm-hearted, much liked, upright, of great ability as a physician and as a man, living in times of change and trouble and danger, he fought a good fight, and has left an honored name.

NOTES

N.B.—Notes are numbered consecutively, and are referred to by their number instead of being repeated.

When not otherwise specified, wills, deeds, etc., are of Morris County record. When any one is known to be living, dates of birth, etc., are not given.

1 Goz-mar, Goth-famous; Goose-mere; written Gozmur, Gosmer, Gosmere, Gosmore, Cosmore, Gosman.

2 In early records the terms "-in-law" or "step-" with father, brother, son, etc., are sometimes omitted; or one is used in the sense of the other.

3 Howell (see Abbreviations).

4 Hist. of the Town and Port of Fordwich, of which a few copies are still obtainable from the author, the Rev. C. Eveleigh Woodruff, M.A., Otterden Rectory, Faversham, Kent (and Editor of the Kent Archæological Society), England.

5 Memorials of the Family of Woodruff, by the Rev. C. E. Woodruff, M.A., for private distribution. Out of print.

6 The parishes of Fordwich, St. Mary Northgate, and Sturry, are contiguous.

7 Register of St. Mary Bredin, Canterbury. Canterbury Marriage Licenses, edited by J. M. Cowper.

8 Canterbury Marriage Licenses, *ut supra*.

9 Hotten's Lists of Emigrants, 1600-1700.

10 Howell, p. 427; S. T. R., I, p. 7.

11 Howell. Hinman's Puritan Settlers; Colonial Records of Conn., 1636-1665. Plymouth Colony Records, IX, 143, 167. Savage's Genealogical Dictionary.

12 Savage's Genealogical Dictionary.

It is possible that this Ann, widow of Richard Carter, was the Ann Woodruff, widow, who, in 1618, married John Gosmer, bachelor (Note 8), who, because the surname was very rare thereabouts, may be believed to have been a son of Mr. Gosmer by a first wife. Widowed a second time, Ann may have married Richard Carter. A third time widowed, it would have been natural for Mr. Gosmer to have provided something out of his wealth for a "kinswoman" who was the widow of his first-born son; and natural for him, when made childless by the death of Richard, to have chosen the name of the dead first-born for his adopted son John.

13 What follows has been taken from the very interesting "Memorials of the Family of Woodruff" (5). If the author would reprint and publish these Memorials he would confer a great boon on all readers.

14 Woodreeve. In the Saxon period in England a reeve "represented the lord of a district, whether township or hundred, at the folkmote (meeting or assembly) of the county; and within his district he levied his lord's dues, and performed some of his judicial functions" (Chamber's Encyclopædia). A "wood-reeve" was presumably reeve for his lord's woodlands. Sometimes written: Woodreefe, Woodrove, Woodroffe, Woodroufe, Woderofe, Woodrofe, Woodrufe, Woodruffe, Woodruff, Woodrow, Woodrop.

15 The only existing Jurats (Channel Islands) are "judges and legislators appointed for life" (Century Dictionary). In Fordwich the Jurat seems to have been Magistrate and Municipal Councillor in one.

16 The Century Dictionary defines "yeoman" as, in recent English use, one owning (and usually himself cultivating) a small landed property; a free-holder. "There came a country gentleman (a sufficient yeoman) to town" (Aubrey. Lives. Walter Raleigh).

17 As, notwithstanding Mr. Woodruff's most careful search of the records, but one adult "John Woodruff" could be found throughout the three parishes,[6] between the years 1625 and 1640, the John Woodroufe who was baptized at St. Mary Northgate in 1604, and was churchwarden at Fordwich in 1632, was, beyond reasonable doubt, the "son John Woodruffe" named in the will of John Woodruffe, 1574-1611, of Northgate; and the baby, John Woodruff, baptized in 1637, in the Parish of Sturry, was presumably the son John who accompanied him to Southampton.

18 S. T. R., II, page 49.

19 Thompson's "Hist. of Long Island"; dedicated to the Honorable Silas Wood. For the above facts stated by Thompson, Savage (Gen. Dict.) refers us to "Wood's History," in which no mention of the name of "Woodruff" has been found.

20 See Note 10. Genealogists have been unable to establish any connection between him and Matthew Woodruff, of Farmington, ancestor of New England family, although both were first on record in America in the same year, 1640.

21 Possibly of the party were also Richard and Ann Carter (see Note 12), who were first on record at Boston, on July 2, 1639 (Drake's Hist. of Antiquities of Boston, page 245). This date may throw light on the time of the arrival in America of the Gosmers and Woodruffs; but, of course, the Carters may have led the way.

22 S. T. R.; W. S. P., I, page 3.

23 The mother, Elizabeth, was first married in 1601.

24 S. T. R., II, page 237.

25 Howell, page 31.

26 S. T. R., I, page 95, Note, and page 155.

27 *Ibid.*, I, page 136. The lot is on the west side of Main Street, nearly opposite, and south of west from, the Gosmer home lot. The house on it, occupied in 1832 by Mr. Frederic Howell (S. T. R., III, Plan), and now by Mr. William Howell, is the one next south of Enoch's millinery store.

28 Howell, page 184.

29 *Ibid.*, page 32.

30 S. T. R., III; Plan of Main Street, Southampton.

31 *Ibid.*, I, page 131. A comparison with the original has shown that

the "John Woodruff" on page 123 of (the published) Vol. I is a misprint for "John Wendall," as, indeed, the context indicates.

32 *Ibid.,* II, page 205.

33 Brand to identify domestic animals.

34 S. T. R., I, pages 149, 150, 151; II, pages 13, 14, 28, 223, 229.

35 *Ibid.,* II, page 222.

36 Howell, page 51.

37 *Ibid.,* page 57.

38 *Ibid.,* page 58. The American "Yorkshire" was made up of Queen's County; King's County, Staten Island, and Newtown; and Suffolk County.

39 S. T. R., II, W. S. P., pages II and III.

40 *Ibid.,* I, pages 150, 151, 152, 175, 179, 180; II, pages 41, 251, 314.

41 *Ibid.,* II, page 350.

42 New York Surrogate's Office, Liber I, folio 69.

43 Anne married Robert Woolley; see Howell, page 408, and S. T. R., II, page 215.

44 Elizabeth married ———— Dayton; probably Robert, son of Ralph. See Howell, pages 229, 230.

45 See Sketch I, end.

46 See Sketch II, end.

47 See Sketches I and II.

48 S. T. R., I, pages 154, 155.

49 *Ibid.,* II, pages 208, 221, 229, 236. The site of the house is now occupied by the residence of Mr. Albert J. Post (Clerk of the Town Trustees), on the east side of Main Street, three doors north of the "Hampton Road" to Bridgehampton, Easthampton, etc.

50 *Ibid.,* II, 218.

51 *Ibid.,* II, pages 8, 223, 225 ("1653" is "1663" in the original record) and 229. The office of constable, even at that time, conferred honor on its occupant, but it was not until 1665 that it was greatly increased in power and dignity by the establishment of "The Court of the Constable and Overseers." S. T. R., II, W. S. P., page II.

52 *Ibid.,* I, page 177.

53 Note 43.

54 S. T. R., II, pages 48, 49 and 236. From a study of the original full text it seems apparent that the exchanges (not sales) of land also registered on these dates, while one or two might have been for the younger brother of the same name, were, in the main, only the putting on record by the emigrant of previous transactions in order to give a good title. In 1679, when living in Etown, he for this purpose confirmed a former sale of land to William Ludlow that seems to have been overlooked at his departure from Southampton. So. Book C of Deeds, folio 338.

55 Hatfield, page 105.

56 The daughter Sarah might have died; and the unmistakable "Sarah" in the original record of Sept. 7th may have been incorrectly copied from a less legible "Mary" in the deed; it is less probable that he remarried in so brief a time.

57 Trenton, Liber D of Deeds, folio 283.

58 The writer is of the Westfield branch of the New Jersey Woodruffs,

descended from the Immigrant through his younger son John, and his son Joseph, as distinguished from the Etown branch, descended through the elder son John he is now writing about.

59 His tombstone, that might tell us, with little doubt lies buried under the turf of the old South End burying-ground. Effort made to ascertain if any of the buried stones of that generation, and later, can be found, proved unsuccessful.

60 The giving of the name "John" to a younger brother while an elder brother also named "John" was still living in the same household, is so unusual it is only reasonable to believe it was not done until the death, in 1649-50, of the step-grandfather's only son, Richard Gosmer (Sketch I) had become a cause for the adoption and the naming. That the younger brother was not included in the arms-bearing list of 1657 is evidence that he was then not 16 years old (S. T. R., I, pages 154, 155). His eldest-born son, John, died prior to 1694;[65] the second of his sons, Joseph, surviving when, on Jan. 4, 1701, he made his will, was not born until 1676 (N. J. Hist. Society Proceedings, Third Series, Vol. II, No. 2, page 115); and the will shows that of his then living children, seven, including all the daughters, were not yet 21 years old. He is, therefore, not likely to have married before 1670, perhaps not until after the death of his father in that year; and if, after the fashion of the times, he married at twenty, or thereabouts, he would have been born about 1650.

61 S. T. R., Orig. Liber A, No. 1, page 57.

62 The use of the word "confirmed" clearly indicates that the deed merely put on record a previous family agreement. The only argument known to the writer against the contention that this former family agreement referred to the younger of the two sons John is the following: On Dec. 18, 1665, Isaac Halsey, in the right as a Proprietor of John Woodruff, Jun., claimed a 300-pound lot,[71][72] and John Woodruff, Sen., a 150-pound lot, of Quagnanantuck (Quaqua, Quogue) land; and on Jan. 19, 1666, they were charged for the lots drawn (S. T. R., I, page 151; II, page 250). When parting with this land in 1672, Mr. Halsey stated (Suffolk Co. Clerk's Office, Small Book of Deeds, page 46) that he had purchased it from "John Woodruff, Jr., the adopted sone of John Gosmer, Gent.," and that this was recorded in a deed (that has not been found) of Sept. 7, 1665; that is, of the very date on which the elder son was selling all his property, prior to his emigration to New Jersey. As, however, Proprietors' rights could only be obtained either by inheritance or by purchase (see Notes 70, 71, 72), and as it is very improbable that either of the two sons had earned money enough to buy rights that would have entitled him to claim a 300-pound lot (the largest amount claimed by any, and by only four, of the Proprietors, and double that claimed by their father), it is reasonable to believe that the 300-pound claim was inherited from Mr. Gosmer. Now, we know that while the parents occupied the homestead after Mr. Gosmer's death, and presumably had a life interest, it was the younger son who, after their death, possessed the homestead, and who willed it, and Mr. Gosmer's other property, to his heirs. Notwithstanding any coincidence of dates, therefore, this seems to prove beyond question that it was he, and not the elder brother, who was the "adopted sone."

Earmark. S. T. R., I, 149. As his father's earmark was "two half-pennys under the left ear," the "one half-penny" had probably been previously used by the elder brother, and abandoned to the younger brother on the former's emigration.

63 Benoni Newton, in a deed of 1682 (So. Red Book of Deeds, folios 77, 78) described John Woodruff as his "brother"; as he had not married either of John's two sisters (Notes 43, 44), "brother" doubtless meant "brother-in-law" (see Note 2) through his own sister. Mr. Newton was a Town Trustee in 1693 (S. T. R., II, 128). "Trustees" were first established by Dongan's Patent, Dec. 6, 1686 (S. T. R., I, Appendix, but omitted in some copies).

64 S. T. R., II, page 63.

65 Ibid., II, page 275. Orig. Liber A, No. 1, folio 101; also No. 2, folio 165. This John was apparently a first-born son, who was not named in his father's will of 1701, because he had died prior to Jan. 8, 1693-4; on which date "John Woodruff records earmark yt was formerly recorded to his son John Woodruff to Samuell Woodruff his son being two half pennys under the left ear" (Ibid., folio 165). In the will, Samuel is named as the "eldest son."

66 Howell, page 44, refers to Doc. Hist. of N. Y., Vol. II, page 536.

67 S. T. R., II, pages 360, 361.

68 Ibid., II, pages 361, 362.

69 Ibid., II, pages 76, 78, 84, 87, 88, 92, 100, 101, 119, 120, 123, 254, 258, 259, 263, 264, 278, 303, 307, 312, 317, 319, 328, 332; So. Liber C of Deeds, folio 37½; So. Red Book of Deeds, folios 338-364.

70 Ibid., I, pages 2 to 6. The accompanying chart, showing the division among the Proprietors of the eastern section of the Town of Southampton, has been adapted from a copy of the original map (kindly loaned by Mr. Orville B. Ackerly), prepared by Mr. William S. Pelletreau, for use in two important Suffolk County suits, 1884-89 and 1891-1900. Mr. Pelletreau's map showed the divisions in completion westward to the Town of Brookhaven.

71 Ibid., I, page 50. Note W. S. P.

72 Ibid., passim, Howell, pages 26 and 27.

73 E. L. I. W., page 261.

74 Howell, pages 60-67; S. T. R., II, W. S. P., pages IV and V.

75 Ibid., page iii.

76 E. L. I. W., page 261.

77 Proceedings, Third Series, Vol. II, No. 2, page 117. He was the progenitor of the Westfield branch of the New Jersey Woodruffs. See Note 58.

78 His lands were situated as follows: Adjoining a pond called Scuttle Hole (about 1½ miles northwesterly from Bridge Hampton); by Long Pond, a string of ponds extending southerly from the above to a point on the "Hampton Road," just west of Bridge Hampton; and Brushey Neck, a part of Hog Neck, lying just west of Sag Harbor's Main Street (S. T. R., II, 90, Note, and 92). The neck is now owned and occupied by Dr. Morton. There was another "Brushey Neck" west of Westhampton (S. T. R., III, page 143). He had lands also adjoining the west side of the Town Pond (Lake Agawam, the Indian name of Southampton), continuing westward,

in Captain's and Halsey's Necks of the Great Plain, and at Shinnecock; northward also at Sebonnucke (Seponnucke, Sebonic, Sebonac), just north of the Golf Grounds. The farm is now in the possession of Captain White. Going westward past Canoe Place, he owned on the Aquebauge (or Accabog) meadows, along the South shore of Great Peconic Bay, south of east from Riverhead. He had previously disposed, by exchange or sale, of other lands at Quogue; at Catchaponak (just west of Quogue meadows); at Sagaponack (Sagg, two or three miles southeast of Bridge Hampton); and of a part of his home lot. For all eastward of Canoe Place see C. and E.

79 S. T. R., III, Plan of Main Street, Southampton.

80 Howell, p. 26.

81 S. T. R., I, pages 150, 151.

82 Letter from Mr. W. S. Pelletreau, of Oct. 19, 1900.

83 So. Liber C of Deeds, folio 827.

84 E. L. I. W., page 261.

85 So. Red Book of Deeds, folio 803, S. T. R., III, page 8.

86 Formerly, many families living outside the villages buried their dead on their own farms, or with their neighbors in a nearby plot. If the land was kept in the family, the graves have been preserved; but in changed hands there might be no one to care for them; and existing tombstones illustrate all the steps of the change from an upright position until only a scrap is still left bare by the ever encroaching sod. In addition, as, for example, at Scuttle Hole, in some instances the entire space is fast being covered by an undergrowth, and at the present pace, before many years have passed, even the memory that it was a burying-ground may be obliterated from the minds of all but a few genealogists.

87 The census of 1776 (S. T. R., III, Appendix) shows that at that time John, Daniel, David, David, Jr., Silas and Benjamin Woodruff were heads of families numbering 26 souls in all. From the order of the list, they were living (apparently not very far apart) to the eastward of Water Mill. There is no evidence that any were living in Southampton or anywhere to the west of Water Mill.

88 See Sketch III, and Proceedings, Third Series, Vol. II, No. 2 (May, 1900), page 115. In his will, John Woodruff (1637-91), first of Etown, named only one son, Joseph. There is abundant evidence (see Hatfield, Index, e. g., page 336) that this son was the Joseph (1674-1746) buried in the Presbyterian graveyard at Etown (Inscriptions, No. 1894); so he of 1676-1742—i. e., born only two years later—could not also have been that John's son. Nor could a Joseph, born 1676, have been his grandson, because his eldest son John's first child was not born until 1683 (Winans). In West Jersey there was a contemporary—a Thomas Woodruff,* of Fenwick's Colony—who also had a son Joseph,* of apparently much the same age as the two East Jersey namesakes; but that Joseph is on record (N. J. Archives, Vol. XXI, pages 617, 629, 632) as a resident of Salem Town, not Westfield. In brief, no New Jersey Woodruff of the period has been found

---

*The line ended with Joseph. Thomas "died having no issue besides his said son Joseph to survive him. . . . Joseph . . . died . . . without issue." T. Deeds, D, pages 218, 219 (Winans).

who could have been either the father or the grandfather of our Joseph Woodruff, Jr., as he was called, doubtless to distinguish him from his only slightly senior Etown cousin. Who, then, was Joseph Woodruff, of Westfield?

In the "List of ye Inhabitants of Southampton, old and young, Christians and Hethen freemen and servants, white and black, Anno 1698" (Howell, page 34), the family of the Etown John Woodruff's younger brother John includes a "Joseph" as the second son. The father, in his will (E. L. I. W., page 261), signed Jan. 14, 1701, bequeathed unto his son "Joseph Woodruffe ye sum of twenty pounds current money of sd Province," and also willed that if either of his sons, Nathaniel or Isaac, "shall depart this life before they come to ye age of twenty-one years then my will is that my son Jonathan Woodruffe shall have his part deceased to him and his heirs forever and if all my sd three sons namely Nathaniel, Isaac and Jonathan shall depart this life without heirs then my will is yt ye aforesd three parcels of land given to them as above be equally divided between my two sons before mentioned namely Joseph and Benjamin and their heirs forever."

Jonathan, who, as above, was to receive (besides twenty pounds when he came of age) only a reversionary interest in his father's lands, was the youngest son, perhaps sixteen years old. As no later mention of him has been found on record, he may have been in ill health, or there may have been some other reason why he, too, was made an exception; but, when every one of the other brothers was left a portion of the father's only too abundant lands, that the second son (Joseph), then over 21, should have been left (besides twenty pounds) only a reversion of the reversionary interests of younger brothers is strong evidence that he was not to remain in his father's neighborhood. That after diligent search no trace of Joseph later than the date of the will has been found in Southampton or Suffolk County further strengthens the probability.

In addition, it should be noted that the final "e" of our surname Woodreeve (14) was retained in Kent down to our emigration in 1639-40. John (1650-1703) of Southampton so retained it in the will above for both himself and his children, including Joseph; and the Westfield defendant was "Joseph Woodruffe" (N. J. Archives, Vol. XIV, page 93). Whereas John (1637-91) of Etown signed his original will (Trenton: Old Essex Wills) "John Woodruff," and his son Joseph also signed without the "e" (Hatfield, pages 247, 284). This later retention (at least until 1719, though afterward dropped) of the "e" by the Westfield Joseph points to New Jersey as the "far country." We know that in the 1699 (for some unknown reason called "Clinker Lot") division many of the settlers of Westfield came from Southampton (Hatfield, page 251); that a "Joseph Woodrufe" drew a lot (Etown Book B; Hatfield, page 307; but see Note 94); that the Joseph who occupied the Westfield lot was, beyond question, the one (1676-1742) buried at Westfield; and that, without reasonable doubt, he was neither son nor grandson of any Woodruff on record as living at that time in New Jersey, but is needed to account for the Long Island son. Taking it by-and-large, therefore, it is evidently safe to believe that the Joseph Woodruffe of Westfield was the Joseph Woodruffe of Southampton.

89 S. T. R., II, page 360.

90 Note 76; Howell, page 408; Hatfield, page 277.

91 Hatfield, pages 80, 241, 242.

92 "Westfields," the rich fields west of Etown (County Histories of Clayton and Ricord).

93 See County Histories. The "church" was at Etown or Woodbridge until, in 1727, Westfield organized one of its own; the first building, however, a log house, not being erected until 1730 (Clayton). While there are no church records extant for the period concerned that might give evidence, there is reason to believe that our Joseph Woodruff was an Elder at both Woodbridge and Westfield (where his eldest son John was a Deacon). Dr. Hatfield, page 358, explicitly referring to the Joseph Woodruff who was the defendant in the Vaughan Ejectment Suit (unquestionably the Joseph of Westfield), states that he was an Elder, but confuses him with his cousin Joseph of Etown, who was also an Elder (of the Etown church); just as on page 582 he made the Joseph of "ten sons" (unmistakably our Joseph, Jr.) a son of that cousin. Similarly, in his Historical Discourse, the Rev. James Huntting (on whom Dr. Hatfield doubtless relied), evidently not aware that there ever was a Westfield Joseph, names as first of their surname at Westfield Joseph's sons John (1704-68) and Jonathan (1707-77), both buried near their father.

One now visiting the well-kept graveyard at Westfield cannot but feel surprised that Mr. Huntting could have failed to see the tombstone of Joseph quite near the front gate; but the surprise vanishes on reading Ricord's statement that by 1865 the old cemetery had become choked by young trees, weeds, vines and berry bushes, so that in Mr. Huntting's time it was doubtless practically impossible to obtain information from the tombstones.

94 See Ill. F (Map). Since the leaflets were published Prof. Samuel R. Winans, of Princeton University, has made (and most kindly shared) very valuable researches, that, while confirming the main statements of the leaflets, interestingly alter some of the details.

For example, from an old deed he has found that it was not the eventual owner, our Joseph Woodruff, Jr., 1676-1742, who, at the 1699 division, drew the Westfield lot No. 149 (see Etown Book B; Dr. Hatfield's "148," on page 307, was doubtless a pen slip, as he places the lot correctly on page 255), but, instead, his Etown cousin, Joseph Woodruff, Sr., 1674-1746 (Note 88), in his right as an Associate. In 1700 Joseph, Jr., was also in Etown (N. J. A., First Series, II, page 334); and no later mention of him there has been found. On Jan. 14, 1701, in good time for his emigration in the spring to Westfield, his father, John Woodruff, at Southampton, made his will (bequeathing Joseph £20) while in "health of body." This, instead of waiting until compelled by the last illness, was so unusual in those days, it plainly indicates a special reason for making the will. On April 1, 1703, the father died, so the £20 would have become available when, on Nov. 15th of that year, Joseph, Sr., and Mary his wife, for £20, conveyed by the old deed to Joseph, Jr., the Lot No. 149, which there is thus reason to believe he had occupied since 1701, under a promise to pay, secured by his father's will.

From two survey maps of 1744, and other old records, Professor Winans further finds that (see Map) Lots 149 and 148 were extended easterly to the river's edge, the northerly section of the former sold, and the northerly section of the latter acquired. So the "Homestead plantation" Joseph, Jr., bequeathed to his sons Thomas and Hezekiah was of both lots. They joined in selling more of 149, leaving about 130 acres for the 1744 partition. Thomas, the same year, sold his share, the lower 20 acres to Hezekiah, to add to his contiguous inherited 65 acres of 148. It is of a part of the latter that Joseph, Jr.'s ownership (by purchase) has been traced from the present (1902) occupants, Mr. and Mrs. Marx Riefel, as follows:

1864. Riefel from Stoddard; Etown; 15; 269.

1859. Stoddard from Miller; Etown; 5; 205.

1859. Miller from Clark, *et als.;* Etown; 4; 237.

(Clark, *et als.,* heirs of Joseph Tooker (Tucker), heir of John Tooker, who died intestate in 1834; see Supreme Court Report of Oct. 29, 1834; Trenton, Book of Partitions, page 281.)

1802. Tooker from Touchembert, Newark F; 409.

1794. Touchembert from Winans, Newark BB; 125.

1784. Winans from Woodruff, Newark F; 339.

The wills (both at Trenton) are:

1776. Stites Woodruff, through Hezekiah Woodruff's will, 20, 37.

1742. Hezekiah Woodruff through Joseph Woodruff's will; C; 475.

Perhaps most satisfactory of all the discoveries is, that on one of the two 1744 survey maps there is a sign indicating a house in 148 where the + is placed in Illustration F; so there need be no doubt that the + approximately marks the site, not only of Hezekiah's home, but also of "my new Dwelling House," named in Joseph, Jr.'s will of Jan. 15, 1742, and told of at the end of Sketch IV.

95 In the 1698 List (Howell, page 34) there were some 34 unmarried (besides married) of the variously spelled name of "Hannah" in a total number of 350 women.

96 The Woodruffs who signed the "Answer" were Samuel; Samuel, Jr.; Thomas; Thomas, Jr.; Cooper; Abner; Robert; Nathaniel; Jacob; Daniel; Abraham; John; John 5th; Joseph; Hezekiah; Jonathan; David; Isaac; Ezekiel; Tim, Jr.; Isaac, Jr.; Jeremiah. Of these, Thomas and Hezekiah certainly, and several of the others probably, were children and descendants of Joseph of Westfield.

97 In October, 1902, this record had apparently not yet been returned to the Supreme Court.

98 N. J. Archives, Vol. XIV, pages 93, 112, 194, 199, 243, 273, 275, 288, 299.

99 The Joseph Woodruff placed on it in 1729 (Hatfield, page 311) was, probably, from his connections with the still unfinished Vaughan Ejectment Suit, the Joseph of Westfield, and not the cousin of Etown.

100 Hatfield; pages 307, 318, 364, 372.

101 Westfield was not set off from Etown as a township until 1794.

102 Trenton, C, 475.

103 Hatfield, page 266.

104 Near the mouth of Rahway River. The modern spelling is perhaps Tremley; and see "Trembly," in Hatfield, pages 267, 509. Until quite recently the inland farmers made annual pilgrimages to the salt meadows by the sea to increase their store of hay.

105 Said to be the modern Morse's Creek, emptying into the Kills near Bayway and Elizabeth. In original will, "Marshes" = Marsh's.

106 Will, Trenton, Liber 18, folio 645.

107 Most of the information here given about the children has been come upon incidentally, but may help in their researches those more closely interested. An asterisk denotes burial in the Westfield gravyard. All wills referred to without special mention are on record at Trenton.

The eldest son (by his tombstone a Deacon), JOHN WOODRUFF,* was born in 1704 and died in Sept., 1768. He lived where Mr. Sylvanus Pierson was living in 1839 (Huntting). His will, I, 341, names wife Elinor, and children John, Moses and Cornelius. JONATHAN* (1707—July, 1777) married, first, Jennet* (1707-50); and second, Prudence* (1709-81). His will, 18-645, names wife Prudence,* children Noah, Aaron, Daniel, Mary (Scudder), Anne (Badgeley). In 1750 he was living a mile north of the Westfield church, at the four corners on the mountain road (County History). WILLIAM married Phebe, daughter of the Joseph Williams of Etown, who died in 1737 (Will, C. C. Gardner, 31, 7, '03). SAMUEL* (1710-54), in his will, F, 208, names wife Elizabeth and daughters (both under 20) Abigail and Rachel. ABIGAIL, wife of John Gold, was born Sept. 12, 1712 (Winans). Of JOSEPH, only what is in the will is known. NATHANIEL, also with details in the will, was born on Oct. 14, 1719 (Maj. Charles E. Woodruff search). THOMAS (1722, June 15—April 2, 1804) married, first, Mary* (1714-53). Anna,* by the inscription, "wife of Capt. Thos. Woodruff, died April 16, 1762, aged 62," it has been found (Winans, Maj. Charles E. Woodruff search) was Ann Scudder, widow of Ephraim Marsh (1700-50), when, on Dec. 6, 1753, she became the second wife. He married, third, on January 31, 1763, Rebekah (1732-1818), by the church records, Rebecca Merry. He was a Judge of Common Pleas (Newark Deeds, F-339). On Dec. 6, 1774, he was appointed a member of the Essex County Committee of Correspondence, or Observation (Clayton, page 64; Hatfield, page 412), and he was otherwise prominent as a patriot. Of HEZEKIAH (1724-76) all that is known is told in Sketch IV. ISAAC married Mary* (1722—Dec. 15, 1766), perhaps the Mary Little by the church records married to Isaac Woodruff, Nov. 19, 1761, or perhaps she was a second wife. The surmise in the leaflets that he might be the Etown Isaac, who died 1803, has been discredited by evidence; and while he, too, may have been of Etown, and have been confused with the other, nothing more is known of him. BENJAMIN was not yet 16 at his father's death. With the Woodruff graves at Westfield there is a "——— (undecipherable), daughter of Benjamin and Jane Woodruff, died May, 1754." By his will (29-533; proved Nov. 27, 1786) he was then of Franklin, Bergen County. He names wife Jane, children Benjamin, Joseph, Joshua, Daniel, Elizabeth and Moses.

By the evidence of the father's will, Thomas, Hezekiah, Nathaniel and Joseph were without "Lawfull Issue" on Jan. 15, 1742.

N.B.—The references to the Westfield church records have been made through the courtesy of Mrs. Henry C. Cooke (H. R. C.), of Westfield (see App. C, 1).

In the office of the Secretary of State, Trenton, N. J. (Essex Co., Files 1730-49) there are copies of Joseph Woodruff, Jr.'s Inventory, dated Feb. 27, 1742, and "Praised" by the "Prisers" Charles Hole and George Ross, respectively Schoolmaster and Wheelwright; and also Executors' Accounts of May 10, 1742. The Accounts show that of the two younger daughters, while Sarah was apparently unmarried (but besides a Sarah Woodruff there were also a Sarah Jefferys and a Caleb Jefferys named), Joanna had become the wife of Josiah Crane. The Inventory includes the "Negro Boy Named Lewye," horses, cattle, sheep, swine, implements, furniture, grain and food in stock, and other belongings, to the value of £304-5-6, which give a glimpse of the household of a well-to-do citizen of the period.

108 The will is dated Oct. 25th, three days later than the date of death on the tombstone, presumably through some error of carelessness.

109 Hatfield; Littell's Passaic Valley; Clayton's Hist. of Union County.

110 Of our ancestor, Dr. HEZEKIAH STITES WOODRUFF, some account is given in Sketch V. For STITES, see Notes 122, 127, 132, 133. For RICHARD, letters of administration (T., 24-22) were granted to the brother, Stites, on Aug. 1, 1780. The will of HIRAM was proved in Middlesex County, March 8, 1820. In Essex County, 1844, letters were issued for a BENJAMIN S. Woodruff, with a widow Hannah; only possibly a son of Hezekiah. For JOHN, see Note 122. For HANNAH Winans and her husband and children, see Appendix C. The will (T. 33-361, 1793) of MARY names nieces Mary Woodruff Winans, daughter of Samuel Winans, and Mary Allwood, daughter of Thomas Allwood, deceased. Of ABIGAIL (Pack), MARGARET and SARAH nothing has been found; but of them, and of all the others, further search would doubtless be rewarded with much information.

111 Sketch IV.

112 *Ibid.*

113 Mrs. Jacob F. Randolph (Maria Louisa Van Lieu), daughter of the Rev. John and Anna Maria (Woodruff) Van Lieu, and granddaughter of Dr. Hezekiah Stites Woodruff, was born Jan. 31, 1831, and died May 27, 1904. In a letter of April 28, 1902, she wrote regarding her grandfather that he was brought up by his uncle, Dr. Stites, of Elizabeth, for whom he was named, and who in his will left him some property. He married Mary, daughter of Dr. Ebenezer Blachly. She is buried in Mendham. His second wife was a widow (Note 146), and mother of Dr. Dufford, who married Harriet, daughter of Dr. Ebenezer Woodruff, the eldest son of our doctor. During the Revolutionary War the grandfather lived at Mine Brook, where he owned a large tract of land, and had a very extensive practice for miles around, including Morristown. A number of wealthy families retained him as their physician by an annual fee. She had heard that he acted as a Surgeon in our army when at and near Morristown. She had not heard of the incident of his supplying cattle to our troops at Valley Forge, but knew that General Washington and General Lafayette had quite often spent the night at the Mine Brook house, her mother having re-

counted to her how her grandmother (Mary Blachly Woodruff) used to tell of their visits, and of thinking them such noble-looking men.

114 T. 35—512, June 28, 1796. HEZEKIAH STITES, son of the Hon. John Stites, 1706-82, was born about 1730; married a daughter of James Patten, who predeceased him, apparently without issue; practiced medicine at Cranbury, Middlesex; joined the Medical Society of New Jersey a year after its foundation, in 1766; was always an influential member, and in 1775 was elected its President; on the erection, in 1785, of the Presbyterian Church at Cranbury, gave the congregation the bell; and died Nov. 17, 1796 (Wickes). It should be recorded in his honor that he bequeathed his negro boy Horace only "until he shall arrive at the age of twenty-one, at which time my will and desire is that he be set free."

115 The total inventory value was over £1,600.

116 One reason for his care of the nephew and namesake may have been that the uncle and mother were full brother and sister by the first wife, Abigail Rushmore, while the others were children of the second wife, Margaret Hampton. Littell, indeed, on page 407, implies that the daughter by the first wife was named "Sarah," but their father, John, in his will, T. 28—436, put Mary Woodruff first and Sarah Gano second, while Littell also states that Mrs. Gano was a daughter of the second wife. This brings back the question, raised in Note 56, whether "Sarah" was not sometimes copied from old manuscript when "Mary" had been written?

117 MARY BLACHLY WOODRUFF was the daughter of Dr. Ebenezer and Mary (Wick) Blachly. Mary Wick was a daughter of Henry and Mary (Cooper) Wick. Mary Cooper was a daughter of Nathan and Mary (Miller) Cooper. See Appendix D.

118 There is no doubt that our great-grandparents lived at "Mine Brook" (113) and owned a "Mine Brook" farm (136). Nowadays, "Mine Brook" would be taken to mean the Lackawanna station of that name, between Bernardsville and Far Hills, or the stream B (Ill. G), and at the end of this note) that gives the name; but careful search has found no deed or tradition to connect them with that neighborhood; while the fact that in the 19th century their son, Dr. Hezekiah Stites Woodruff (born 1795), for a time lived beside the stream at Far Hills (then the Lesser Cross Roads) may have caused confusion. On the other hand, there is much to connect them with the Washington Corner district and its little "Mine Run," A (Ill. G; apparently also sometimes spoken of as "Mine Brook"); so known from at least as early as 1746 (H-122), and so named from an iron mine (never worked) beside it.

In 1779 Samuel Lewis bought (A-275) from Joseph Byram 36½ acres in Mendham township. This lot, together with two similar lots (and the promise of a money payment), he, in 1781, conveyed (W-335, not recorded until 1812) to Dr. Woodruff in exchange for the latter's "farm at Mine Brook" (see Note 136), the deed for which has not been found. A lawsuit delayed this 1781 transaction until 1788, when it was settled (136) by Lewis conveying back the farm, with a lessened money payment, and Woodruff conveying back two out of the three lots.

On Dec. 24, 1791, Dr. Woodruff sold (B-286; recorded Feb. 14, 1794) to Dr. William Leddell, his wife's uncle, 105 acres in the township of

Mendham, "or near the border thereof." On Sept. 7, 1792, Dr. Leddell sold to Japhet Byram 36¾ acres in Mendham to., which, from the courses described in the three 1779, 1781 and 1792 deeds being identical, is unmistakably the Lewis-Woodruff-Leddell lot. This, subtracted from the 1791 Woodruff-Leddell 105 acres, would leave 68¼ acres in Mendham to., or "near the border thereof"; that is, or "over the border in Bernard," to which to. our doctor was assigned in the Lewis deed and lawsuit. The boundaries in the 105 acres deed are vague, but "Brogden's line" passed through the mouth of "Mine Run" (H-122), and the inherited lands of Major Henry Axtell "in the neighborhood" were not far on the other side of the Mendham-Basking Ridge road, shown in the map and the plan opposite. All this points to the present Mrs. Hannah Coleman, part Mendham part Bernard, property (Ill. G) as the 68¼ acres not accounted for.

Her attractive property, now containing 75 acres (B-4—146), in 1833 (D-3—206) was of "70 acres more or less," which, for those days, was near enough to the 68¼ figures. Its ownership has been traced further back (F-3—98; S-2—89) to heirs, in 1823, of Preserve Riggs (a friend and neighbor of the two Doctors, both much given to buying and selling land, so he may easily have bought it from Dr. Leddell); whose possessions (Ill. G, 10) touched the Coleman property at the northeast, while the more southerly contiguous Leddell homestead (Ill. G, 11) lands came up to the bank of Mine Run, which stream (Ill. G, A) forms so much of the northeasterly-easterly boundary of the Coleman property it would have been natural to call that the "Farm at Mine Run," or even the "Farm at Mine Brook." Further, the Blachly lands (Ill. G, 3, 4) then extended southward to parts of the northern limits of the farms of both Mrs. Coleman and Mr. Oliver Sanders (Ill. G, 2).

The latter's farm, which is part of the southwesterly boundary of the former, and the northerly boundary of the property of Thomas S. Ormiston, Esquire, was (together with a piece on the other side of the road) sold (V-2—275) by Dr. Woodruff to William Guerin in 1827. The record of the successive conveyances down to Mr. Sanders is complete; but no record has been found of the doctor's purchase of either of the two properties (both may have then been Blachly lands), although he thus certainly owned this Guerin-Sanders farm, which, as the plan opposite shows, seems to have been a fragment from the larger property that had given the Mine Run family needed access to the road leading to the parents' home (Ill. G, 3, 4).

Considering the above, and what we know of the doctor's life during the Revolution, it seems fair to conclude that the "farm at Mine Brook" was at the "Mine Run" brook. In addition, while the "Riggs house" proper (Ill. G, 10), built by Preserve Riggs, and now owned by Miss Denton (App. E; 5 and 6), is at Washington Corner, the one on the Coleman farm was so long occupied by members of the Riggs family, and the Woodruff stay was so far back, and so brief, that it, too, is naturally called the "Riggs house." For decades, however, it has been known as of the "over a hundred years" class, and, from its construction, was doubtless standing in 1776, to be the first home of the young couple.

It may be added that from tradition it is likely our doctor owned other lands near by, of which the record has been lost. For example, Mr. Henry Sutton (died Oct. 25, 1904), in August, 1903, remembered his father having told him that long ago our great-grandfather lived on the present Mr. and Mrs. William Thompson farm (Ill. G, 9), bounding him both sides of the road on the west. The Suttons bought their land, and built the house still standing, in 1796, so it is quite possible that on our doctor's return from Pennington to Mendham, in 1792 (139) he occupied the Thompson property for some years; but the earliest record found is that of its sale (C-3—488) in 1799 by his brother-in-law, Absalom Blachly. From its

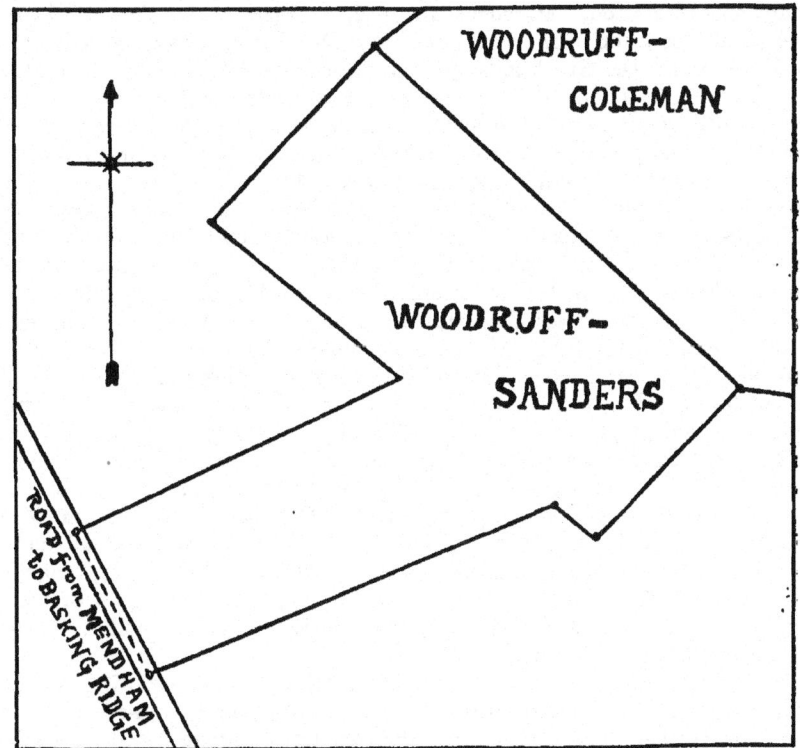

situation it presumably had been Blachly property; it may have been that it was presented to the young couple on their marriage, and by them subsequently sold to Absalom.

Reverting to the modern Mine Brook (Ill. G, B), Gordon's Gazeteer (1834) describes it as a mill stream of great force, studded with mills (now gone), that rises near Logtown, on the summit of Mine Mount, and runs six miles southwest into the Raritan. Logtown (Ill. G, 16), later sometimes called Reynoldsville, or Greenville, at that time consisted of a fulling-mill on a stream flowing into the Passaic (both the mill and its frame dwelling house being now in ruins), and three or four other houses (the stone house at the corner was originally the stable of the mill property opposite); and as a matter of fact, the longest branches of Mine Brook rise at some distance from it on Mine Mount, but on the way from Bernardsville (Vealtown) to Logtown there is a noteworthy spring, that, when the mountain was less traveled, might have been considered the main source of the brook.

119 Sketch IV.

120 In a letter of Nov. 28, 1898, to the writer, the late Mr. William S. Cary, of Cary's Station, Flanders, N. J., a very old friend of the family, wrote that he had no positive proof that our great-grandfather was a surgeon in the army, but as a boy used to hear him spoken of as having occupied that station. Moreover, in 1832, or 1833, in his father's house, a surgical operation was performed (by Dr. Jacob Drake Woodruff, a grandson, under Dr. Hezekiah's eye), so light there were lookers-on, including himself, but sufficient to cause one of them to tumble over. Joking him for his weakness, Dr. Hezekiah said he would make a very poor soldier, but might get over it after dressing the wounds of as many soldiers as the doctor had dressed. See also 113 and 143.

121 For example, his brother-in-law, Dr. Ebenezer Blachly, Jr., 1760-1812, appears in the records concerned only as Ebenezer Blackly, Surgeon's Mate on the roll of the 10th North Carolina for July, 1778; but from the recorded knowledge of his contemporaries (see Wickes, page 150) it is known that at least he was also attached as volunteer surgeon to a regiment of the Pennsylvania line; wintered at Valley Forge (where his brother Absalom visited him, as by his published notes; Wickes); and served at the battles of White Plains, 1776, and Monmouth, June, 1778. His tombstone at Pennington, where he died while on a visit from Paterson to his brothers, records him as an "officer in the war for American Independence." See also History of Bergen County, Clayton, page 359, and Note 139.

122 T. Book 172 of Damages done by the British, 1776-1782, and never paid for. When the return was called for in 1789, Stites Woodruff added the item, "1 very good Large Mare plundered 29th July, 1781, £35," making his total loss £67. The word "plundered" points to an incursion of "cowboys" from Staten Island, who were very active in 1781, until Yorktown fell (Hatfield, pages 501-6).

From the wording of their father Hezekiah's will (T. 20-37), and for other reasons, this brother Stites has been mistakenly regarded as our great-grandfather (also commonly called "Stites Woodruff"), Dr. Hezekiah Stites Woodruff; among the "other reasons" being that H. S. W. seemed to be considered the head of the family, when, for example, on Aug. 24, 1787, Gov. William Livingston granted him letters of guardianship (T. Wills, 29-299), and on April 23, 1799 (T. Wills, 38-40) he was made administrator of the estate of the youngest brother, John. (See also Notes 110, 136.) However, a later found record (Dr. Cory, App. C), viz., the marriage, at or near New Providence, N. J., on June 8, 1774, of a Stites Woodruff to a Sarah Miller (H. S. W. having married Mary Blachly on May 11, 1776), makes the wording of the will more clear, and leaves no reasonable doubt that there were two contemporary brothers known as "Stites Woodruff." That the later found Stites was the elder of the two seems probable from the fact that H. S. W. was not born until his father was some thirty years of age, while it was Stites, not H. S. W., who, in 1780, was made administrator (110) for their brother Richard, and Stites and Sarah who, after the division of the father's property, inherited, and in 1784 conveyed the Westfield homestead (94). No will or letters of administration have been found. Presumably, also, it was S. W., not H. S. W., who was the father (Littell, page 169) of Abigail (Abby) Woodruff (1789—July 20, 1836, buried in Springfield, N. J.), married in 1806 to William Halsey. (See Thomas Halsey and His Descendants in America.)

123 He grew up to be the well-known Dr. Ebenezer Blachly Woodruff, I, of Drakesville (Ledgewood) and Succasunna, and to be the son who was the stay of the father in his last days.

124 Gordon's New Jersey, page 263.

125 The statement rests on a letter of July 7, 1902, from the late Mrs. George B. Selden (Clara Drake Woodruff; App. B), of Rochester, N. Y., whose father, Dr. Jacob Drake Woodruff, of Brooklyn, N. Y., son of Dr. E. B. Woodruff, I, told her that after the death of Hezekiah Stites Woodruff in 1842, the grandsons, Dr. Jacob among them, looked through his papers and destroyed those they considered of no value, including this letter from General Washington. The sentence, "For God's sake send me some cattle; my men are starving," burned itself on his memory. He also told her of the mortgage and other details in the text; and besides, that the claim against our government is recorded at Washington—unpaid.

126 See Dr. McClintock's most valuable address, before the Washington Association of New Jersey, "Topography of Washington's Camp of 1780, and its Neighborhood," 1894.

127 Through the courtesy of the Adjutant-General's Office at Trenton it is known that there was a Stites Woodruff who served as a private from Dec. 3, 1780, to Jan. 1, 1781, in Capt. Benjamin Laing's company of the First Regiment, Essex County, New Jersey Militia. It is also stated (Newark Evening News Jersey Genealogy, 642) that a Stites Woodruff, on June 30, 1776, was on the muster roll of Captain Richard Townley's company. He was probably the brother of our great-grandfather referred to in Note 122 and the text.

128 Dr. McClintock's Address, page 13. General Wayne having accompanied his mutinous soldiers toward Pennsylvania, his baggage was left in care of Dr. Blachly, the father-in-law (Ill. G, 3).

129 The date of the removal is assumed to have been between the sale of his former home, Dec. 26, 1781, and the date, April 12, 1783, when he executed a mortgage deed (Flemington records) for his Pennington farm lands (131). The deed conveying to him the new homestead has not been found, but from his own later deed of sale (T., A T-189) it is known to have been of some 23 acres, with a frontage on the main street (to Trenton) a short distance south from the Presbyterian Church, and graveyard, which at the rear it enveloped, reaching to the cross street (to Princeton). Under later owners the frontage was widened and part of the land at the rear transferred to the graveyard; but the site was substantially that owned and occupied in 1902 by Miss Margaret Fish. His house was near the street, but when his successor built the fine old mansion, still standing, at

a dignified distance back, our doctor's house was retired to serve as a suplementary building, and has been long gone. Besides the evidence of the deed of sale, through the kindness of Maj. Jno. G. Muirheid the writer met Aaron S. Laning, Esquire, over 80 years old, and devoted to the history of the long ago. His authority for the above statements was confirmed by the many others who kindly supplied information.

130 At Princeton, on May 4, 1784, he was made a member of the Medical Society of New Jersey; was present at the annual meetings, 1785, '88, '90; and in 1787 was appointed one of the examiners to inquire into the qualifications of licentiates. After 1796 his name does not appear on the records, perhaps because Mendham was so much farther away from Princeton than the convenient Pennington, and because, with his father-in-law's extensive practice, he was too busy. It may here be added that on June 22, 1825, he was elected an honorary member of the Morris County Medical Society, founded 1816.

131 On April 12, 1783, he executed a mortgage deed (Flemington records) to Benjamin Kitchen for some 43 acres of village and farming lands; with the proviso that if within one year he did not repay the £553 Proclamation money, received in cash, the deed become absolute.

132, 133 Contrary to previous belief, it was doubtless the brother, Stites Woodruff (see Note 122), not our doctor, who, to repay the executor concerned £198 he had borrowed from Joseph Jelf (see Note 134), on July 27, 1783, mortgaged (Newark; Mortgages, A-525) to their uncle, Thomas Woodruff, a part of his Westfield inheritance adjacent to the also inherited homestead he, on April 4, 1784, sold to Jacob Winans (Newark; Deeds, F-339; Note 94). About the time of this sale he repaid the uncle, and the mortgage was canceled.

134 Joseph Jelf, in 1757, was of full age, and had been clerk and bookkeeper upward of three years for the Hon. Samuel Woodruff (died 1768) of Elizabethtown. Soon after he became his partner in business. (Hatfield, pages 338-9.) He married a daughter of Jonathan Hampton (116, and text).

135 Gordon, Hist. of N. J., page 301.

136 Of the suits at the Supreme Court, Trenton, in which Dr. Woodruff was plaintiff, the record enclosed in Hunterdon and Somerset County Envelope No. 45, 443, tells that in Dec., 1781, he conveyed "his farm at Mine Brook" (Note 118) to Samuel Lewis, in exchange for three (Deeds, W-335) lots and a money promise of £800. Failing payment, in 1786 there was a judgment, also not paid, followed by an arbitration. By this Lewis was to pay £450, instead of the £800, and return the farm, and Woodruff to return two of the three lots. In 1787 a payment was made, but in 1788 further action (Hun., 46, 545) was required to complete the settlement.

Apparently the trouble was to determine a fair money equivalent in fluctuating currency, and it was the same, probably, with the (Morris, 45, 445) £350 debt of Dr. William Leddell; with the $633 found (Hun., 44, 116) still due on the £1,000 debt of Dr. Henry W. Blachly, and with others (Som., 45, 622; 43, 919; 44, 755).

Further suits were (Mor. 44, 111) Abel Cary land to be sold for debt of £351 (see Note 142); for (Hun., 45, 621) failure to keep harmless from a mortgage, £4,000. After 1800 there were (Mor., 44, 379) an ejectment suit to protect purchaser or lessee; one (Mor. 45, 444) with other plaintiffs to recover $75, apparently in some town matter. Suits were brought, in 1792 (Essex, 45, 624) as guardian (Note 122) for his younger brother John; and in 1819 (Mor., 45, 623), as executor of Michael Ehle. Envelopes, Som., 44, 381; 44, 562; 44, 372; contain too scanty details to be intelligible.

137 History of Burlington and Mercer, Woodward and Hageman, 1883, page 825. The History adds that Dr. Woodruff "was followed by Dr. Henry W. Blachly, who was very successful, and soon went to New York for his brother Absalom, a law student, who dropped Blackstone and took up the study of Physic." These two brothers of the doctor's wife, viz., Henry Wick, 1763-1813, and Absalom, 1765-1834, remained at Pennington, and are buried there.

138 T., A T-189.

139 The eldest son, Dr. Ebenezer Blachly, Jr., 1760-1812, who would naturally have been his father's successor, had been weaned away by his army service (121), and his marriage to Elizabeth, daughter of the gallant Colonel Spencer, so had gone from home to live in Paterson (B-238, P. A., Feb. 24, 1791, to his brother Absalom for his Morris Co. lands, etc.; Note 140; Hist. Bergen Co.). Drs. Henry and Absalom, provided for by our doctor's departure from Pennington, seem to have been unmarried. William, just when his medical studies were about completed, died on Jan. 30, 1791, in his twenty-third year. The other children were still young. So the lot fell to our great-grandparents.

140 Miss Mary E. Leddell, at the Leddell homestead (Ill. G, 11), has kindly told the writer that the Blachly "mansion-house" (Ill. G, 3), within a few years still standing. had behind its two ground-floor front rooms a large hall, with lofty ceilings, commanding a fine view. The site can still be recognized by the yellow lilies that took the place of turf on the street side. She has also supplied the interesting advertisement herewith: "For sale. In a body or in three or more lots, The Farm, late of E. Blachly, Senior, of 300 acres in Mendham. It has about 50 acres of fine bottom Meadow, and 30 more may be made, about 80 acres of woodland—200 apple trees besides other fruit trees, a mansion-house, outhouses and two other dwelling-houses, etc.

"The farm is well watered, and in fence, 100 yards from a distillery, half-a-mile from an academy and church, in a good neighborhood, a healthy situation—only 30 miles from New York. For terms apply to E. Blachly at Paterson; H. W. Blachly, Pennington; A. Blachly, Mendham; or C. C. Blachly, Succasunna; by whom a good title will be given, and terms of payment made easy to the buyers." From the New Jersey Journal, "Elizabeth-town; Printed and Published by Shepard Hollock, every Tuesday, at Two dollars per Annum. Advertisements of a moderate length inserted Three Weeks for Eight Shillings, and two shillings for each insertion afterwards."

141 The Blachly property was sold to Peter and Ann Elizabeth DeGroot (T., 4, 86); DeGroot released title to his father-in-law, Abraham Banker, on Sept. 24, 1818 (G-2, 519).

142 The Hill Top homestead (Ill. G, 6) was bought (T-151) from Jonathan Dayton, and can be traced back (T-284, 292) only to Benjamin and Elizabeth Beach (P-217) in 1808, who perhaps inherited it. Its 5 33-100 acres are bounded N. by Prospect St. (once The Lane; later Seminary St., from Dr. Rankin's school); E. by Church St.; S. and W. by the property of Elisha Beach (perhaps a descendant of Benjamin). The latter is now owned by Miss Eliza D. Thompson, who kindly pointed out the boundary marks named in the above deeds; all of which, after temporary partitions, now coincide with those of the present Dr. La Lasure homestead.

Our doctor's further dealings in real estate were considerable. On June 20, 1810, he conveyed (V-70) to his son, Dr. W. P. Woodruff, 158 acres in Mendham to.; a part of the S. W. boundary being "the long line," which with surveyors means "Dunstar's line." A study of the deeds and the maps makes it fairly clear that these 158 acres were a part of 200 acres from the Charles Dunstar tract (3,500 acres, Dec. 27, 1721), lapping over from Bernard into Mendham to.; which was conveyed in 1778 (A-5) to Abel Cary; sold by Supreme Court order (136, Morris, 44, 111) for debt of £351; and in 1791 deeded (V-307) as 150 acres, for £351, by Sheriff William Leddell to our doctor. It passed out of the family when Dr. W. P. Woodruff parted with it in April, 1811.

In 1810, also, the doctor bought (T-276) 33 acres of farm land apparently starting northwesterly from the high road (near the Blane place), between Mendham and Roxiticus (Ralston), which he sold (Y-2, 556) on Jan. 1, 1830. Still in 1810, on July 5, he bought (T-329) 7 17-100 acres on the south side of West Main St.; 3 4-10 acres of which, just east of New St. (Ill. G, 8) he sold (C-3, 69) on May 12, 1832 (148). In 1811, 20 acres inherited from the mother-in-law, Mary Blachly, were sold (V-311). All through his stay at Mendham there were dealings in land with John Marsh, Hannah Blachly, Henry Pierson, William Guerin, and many others; as is shown by the record, on which, even after he had gone to Succasunna, his name still appeared.

143 The "Genius of Liberty," Morristown, N. J., 1824, June 26; 1825, June 23. The files at the Morristown Library are not complete, and the issues one would most like to consult are too often missing.

144 His son, Dr. Absalom (with a son also a doctor), following him at Mendham, "old Dr. Woodruff" came in time to apply to two men, but while they were alike kindly, and greatly esteemed, the son was as grave and deliberate as the father was cheery and impulsive. So it is easy to tell which is meant even when the wrong name has been given.

145 Mary Blachly Woodruff died between Dec. 13, 1822, and 1826; but the exact date is not known. See Appendix D.

146 Elizabeth Hager was born in 1778; as widow of Jacob Dufford, became the second wife of Dr. H. S. Woodruff in 1826, and died Feb. 14, 1866. Buried first at Schooley's Mountain, in the Dufford homestead burial plot, on the sale of that farm the coffin, with others, was removed to Naughright, N. J. Her son, Dr. William Dufford, married Harriet, daughter of her stepson, Dr. E. B. Woodruff, 1778-1852.[118]

147 The Rev. Theodore L. Cuyler, D.D., LL.D., himself a widely known and very distinguished graduate of the Ezra Fairchild "Hill Top" school,

wrote of it (Jan. 4, 1904) that in the time of Ezra Fairchild's management it was regarded by the Faculty of Princeton College as one of the best of the New Jersey schools, being so thorough in its classical and mathematical departments that the students it sent to Princeton came there more than ordinarily well prepared. The school is also well spoken of in T. F. Gordon's, and a picture of the school building (and the church) is shown on page 383 of Barber's, History of New Jersey.

Among the "Hill Top boys" were Vice-Chancellor Henry C. Pitney, of Morristown, who is too well known to need particulars (excepting that it may here be said that to anything of interest there may be in Sketch V he has kindly added his full share); the Hon. Henry M. Fuller, of Pennsylvania, who received many votes in Congress for the Speaker's chair; Rev. L. D. Potter, President of Glendale Female College, Ohio; Rev. Aaron R. Wolfe, of Montclair, N. J., author of most excellent hymns; Mr. B. H. Howard, of Alabama; and several others who obtained honorable positions in life.

After Mr. Fairchild removed his scholars to Plainfield, and the property passed into the hands of Mr. Galloway, it soon ceased to succeed as a school, and the building was thereafter used as a dwelling, etc., until it was torn down. The foundations can still be seen in the Dr. La Lasure grounds.

148 This property he did not sell (C-3, 69) until May 12, 1832, although the "of Roxbury to.," equivalent to "Succasunna," in the deed (Y-2, 556) conveying his 33-acre farm (T-276) indicates that he had ceased to be "of Mendham to." prior to Jan. 1, 1830 (see Note 142).

149 Munsell's History of Morris County, page 245; but see Note 144.

150 His will (G-98), after providing for his wife, left his lands to be sold and divided among his children; but since its writing, in 1833, there had been changes, including the sale of the Virginia lands he therein devised. These ten thousand acres on Cheat River, in Randolph County, Virginia (now West Virginia; County Clerk at Elkins), were, on Nov. 9, 1795, granted to Richard Smyth; who, in 1799, sold them to Dr. Samuel Robinson. The latter had been adjudged debtor to Dr. Hezekiah Stites (114, 115, 116) who died before the judgment was satisfied. His executors, our doctor being both an executor and a beneficiary, accepted the above lands as security; and our doctor's son, Dr. E. B. Woodruff, was appointed assignee by the Court. In 1804 our doctor bought the property at the public sale; and in 1837 sold it to his son, Dr. E. B. Woodruff. He, after the father's death, sold it, in 1845, to his brother, Dr. W. P. Woodruff, then of Barbour Co., but so later of Randolph Co., Virginia (Randolph Co., W. Va.; 5-324; 5-326; 13-180; 1845—Liber and folio not supplied). The latter occupied the place for a time, but it passed out of the family when he went West. See Appendix B, where something is told of our great-grandfather's children, and of some of their descendants.

APPENDIX

THIS miscellaneous material is preserved here in order that it may be useful to the coming genealogist. When any one is known to be living, dates of birth, etc., are not given.

APPENDIX A

THE MOTHERS

(*See page* 1)

GEN.	NAME.	CHIEF HOMES.	MARRIAGE.
I.	Unknown	Fordwich	About 1508
II.	Unknown.	"	" 1536
III.	Alice Russell	"	1573
IV.	Elizabeth Cartwright	" , So'ampton	1601
V.	Anne ———	" "	About 1635
	ETOWN BRANCH.		
VI.	Mary Ogden	Southampton, Etown	" 1659
	WESTFIELD BRANCH.		
VI.	Hannah Newton	Southampton	" 1670
VII.	Hannah ———	So'ampton, Westfield	" 1700
VIII.	Mary Stites	Westfield	" 1744
	(H. S. W. Branch.)		
IX.	Mary Blachly	Mendham	1776
	(Note to App. B.)		
X.	Eliza Drake	Succasunna	1814
XI.	Elizabeth Sophia Coursen	N. Y. City, Morristown	1838
XII.	Elizabeth Mills	Glen Ridge	Living

APPENDIX B

HEZEKIAH STITES WOODRUFF'S CHILDREN;

and some of their descendants

THE members of the family are indebted for what follows to Philemon Woodruff, Esquire, of East Orange and Newark, who gave the writer his "start" in compiling these sketches. The arrangement has been adopted, by memory, from Mr. Fred. A. Canfield's Canfield Genealogy.

Trace through figures following name; for example, the descent from IX, Dr. Hezekiah Stites Woodruff, of XIII, 14. Edward Coursen Woodruff, 40, is through XII, 39-40, Edward Coursen Woodruff, 16; XI, 16, Ebenezer Blachly Woodruff, 5; X 5, Absalom Woodruff. Asterisks refer to Note at end of this Appendix (B). Additions to original draft are put out of order at end of generation concerned; for example, XIII, 22, Henry Rogers Selden, 7, is separated from XIII, 2, Clara Sayre Selden, 7.

GENERATION X. 1. EBENEZER BLACHLY W., M.D., b. Sept. 22, 1777, at Mine Run (Note 118); m. about 1805; passed his grown life at Drakesville (Ledgewood), where, and at the neighboring Succasunna, he practiced his profession; part of the time in partnership with his younger brother, Absalom; the two having m. sisters. On July 2, 1816, he was made a mem. of the Morris County Medical Society (founded June 11, 1816); and on July 5, 1820, was elected its President (presumably he was also a mem. of the Medical Society of New Jersey). He d. June 15, 1852. He m. (1) Clarissa Drake, dau. of Col. Jacob Drake (App. D), who gave its name to Drakesville. The w. was b. Aug. 23, 1783, and d. March 31, 1837. Both are bur. at Succasunna. 2. RICHARD W., b. Aug. 21, 1780; d. Jan. 17, 1785. 3. HARRIET W., b. Jan. 18, 1782; d. in her fifth year. 4. WILLIAM PATERSON W., M.D., b. March 23, 1785. Between, say, 1810-20, his home, neighboring New

Vernon, N. J., was some 300 yards from the present Van Doren's Mills, on the road to Logtown (Ill. G) and Bernardsville. He practiced also at Paterson and Milford (Hunterdon Co.). In 1840 he filed a certificate with the Mor. Co. Medical Society that his son, Absalom B. W., began the study of medicine with him on Jan. 9, at German Valley. In 1845 he was described in a deed as of Barbour Co., Virginia; and by the purchase became next of Randolph Co., Va. (Note 150). He d. at Mount Pleasant, Ohio (Hist. Bergen Co., N. J.). His wife was Leah V. W. 5. ABSALOM W., M.D., m. (1) 5 Eliza Drake; m. (2) 6 Elizabeth Riggs; m. (3) 7 Joanna Nitel Johnes.* 8. HEZEKIAH STITES WOODRUFF, M.D., b. July 4, 1795; lived and practiced at the Lesser Crossroads (now Bedminster), Bernard to., before and after 1840; was living in Newark about 1846; later, for a year or so, rented the property near Roxiticus (Ralston), Mendham to., now the St. John's Church summer home for children. He removed to Lafayette, Sussex Co., but apparently (Snell's Sussex Co.) d. at Newark, where his widow was living in 1898 (now dec'd). He was m. at least twice. His (perhaps second) wife was Eliza, dau. of Robert Thompson, judge and farmer in Sussex Co. 9. ANNA MARIA W., b. Jan. 2, 1800; m. the Rev. John VAN LIEU, of Readington, N. J.

GENERATION XI. 1. HARRIET W., 1, b. April 23, 1806 (deceased); m. Dr. William DUFFORD (Note 146). 2. JACOB DRAKE W., 1, M.D., b. July 30, 1808; m. Oct. 2, 1837, Harriet Tomlinson Sayre, of Morristown, N. J. (who d. at Drakesville, N. J., March 23, 1849); was proposed by his brother John and admitted mem. the Mor. Co. Med. Society, May 5, 1834; on committee to obtain names unlicensed practitioners; Jan. 7, 1836, on committee to revise by-laws; June 6, 1837, delegate to State meeting Med. Soc'y of N. J. He was later the well-known Dr. Jacob W. of Brooklyn, N. Y., where he d. Feb. 12, 1877. 3. ELIZA ANNE W., 1, b. Feb. 18, 1811 (deceased); m. Charles J. HOPKINS. 4. GEORGE K. DRAKE W., 1, b. May 31, 1813; d. Dec. 27, 1887; m. Mary Green (deceased). 5. ADELINE W., 1, b. Jan. 12, 1816 (deceased); m. Samuel I. GUSTIN, d. in Georgia in 1873. 6. JOHN B. W., 1, M.D., b. April 13, 1818. His father presented certificate to Mor. Co. Med. Society that John began the study of medicine with him on Nov. 16, 1833; d. March 3, 1903, in Chicago; m. Margaret Bartlett in 1840, she d. in 1902. 7. SOPHIA E. W., 1, b. Sept. 22, 1821; d. Sept. 8, 1841, aged twenty years. 8. CORNELIUS

BLACHLY W., 1, b. Dec. 10, 1824; d. in California, April 23, 1861, unmarried. 9. MARY BLACHLY W., 1, b. March 10, 1828; d. in Newark, N. J., in 1899; m. Rev. J. Kirby DAVIS (deceased). 10. HEZEKIAH STITES W., 4. 11. WILLIAM B. W., 4, left children, but all traces lost. 12. LEAH ANN W., 4, m. Asa CARY, brother of Alice and Phebe Cary, authoresses. 13. LOUISA W., 4, m. —— RUNYON. 14. ABSALOM B. W., 4 (deceased), was b. at New Vernon, Morris Co., N. J. (See Clayton's Bergen Co. Hist.), July 9, 1819; was in business; studied medicine with his father two years; was admitted to the bar, Attorney 1844, Counsellor 1847. On April 26, 1849, m. 14, Isabella (dau. of Gen. George D'Wolf, of Bristol, L. I., and later Cuba), who d. Sept., 1856; was appointed Col. First Regt. Passaic Brigade; was prosecutor of the pleas for many years, until made President Judge of Court of Common Pleas. He was a leader in politics and city affairs, and a man of mark. 15. HENRY W., 4, a lawyer, of New York City and Washington, D. C.; m. Annie Stickney (See XII, 53, 54, 55). 16. EBENEZER BLACHLY W., M.D., 5, m. 16 Elizabeth Sophia Coursen.* 17. ABSALOM BLACHLY W., 5, b. 1816; d. June 25, 1849, unmarried. 18. ABSALOM FRANKLIN W., 5, b. 1816; d. Oct. 12, 1822. 19. MARY ANN W., 5, b. Feb. 14, 1819; d. March 14, 1819. 20. ELIZA ESTHER W., 5, b. Feb. 15, 1820; m. (1) Oct. 19, 1841, Edward W. WHELPLEY (Chief Justice of N. J.); m. (2) 1867, David Stuart DODGE; d. May 25, 1895. 21. MALE INFANT, 7, d. Nov. 24, 1839. 22. ANNA MARIA W., 8, m. Clarkson DRAKE, of Newark, N. J., and d. w. i. 23. JULIA W., 8, m. Martin B. PROVOST, of Newark, N. J., and has three children. 24. LOUISA W., 8, m. Robert GRAY, Jr., of Newark, N. J., and has two children. 25. ROBERT T. W., 8, d. 1904; m., and left one child. 26. EMMA W., 8, m. Edward ELVERSON, of Newark, N. J., now deceased, and has three children; has recently remarried. [Snell's Sussex Co. states that X-8 had four sons; one of the same name, and also a physician, succeeding him at Lafayette, removing to Marksboro', and dying March 29, 1858.] 27. CORNELIUS S. VAN LIEU, 9, m. (1) 27, Sarah, dau. of David Oakes, of Bloomfield, N. J., and (2) 28, Susan Moore. 29. MARIA LOUISA VAN LIEU, 9, b. Jan., 1831; m. Oct. 18, 1853, Jacob Fitz RANDOLPH (1828-1897); d. May 26, 1904. 30. JOHN NEWTON VAN LIEU, 9, m. Dora Kuhl, and d. about ten years ago (1905).

Generation XII. 1. THEODORE DUFFORD, 1, d. in 1898, at Newark, N. J., leaving a widow, now deceased, but no children. 2. CLARISSA DUFFORD, m. (1) James WOODRUFF; (2) ———— KISSAM; d. at Newark in 1887, w. i. 3. MARY DUFFORD, 1, wife of Thomas J. HARRISON, has two children. 4. CHARLOTTE TOMLINSON W., 2, unmarried, Rochester, N. Y. 5. HARRIET BENEDICT W., 2, b. Aug. 6, 1840; d. Jan. 6, 1848. 5-a. NOAH BENEDICT W., 2, b. July 15, 1842; d. Feb. 3, 1845. 6. SAMUEL SAYRE W., 2, b. June 15, 1844; lived at Charleston, W. Va.; d. Brooklyn, L. I., March 21, 1877. 7. CLARA DRAKE W., 2, b. March 5, 1846; m. Dec. 14, 1871, George Baldwin SELDEN, of Rochester, N. Y.; d. Oct. 7, 1903; she knew much, and gave much of the history of our family. 7-a. BENEDICT W., 2, b. May 13, 1848; d. in Charleston, W. Va., in 1879. 8. RIENZI HOPKINS, 3, in war for Union; lawyer; m. and with children. 9. WALTER HOPKINS, 3, in war for Union; lawyer; m. and with children. 10. GEORGE GREEN W., 4, b. Feb. 17, 1843; d. Aug. 19, 1844. 11. KATHARINE TENEYCK W., 4, unmarried. 12. SOPHIA W., 4 (deceased), b. Dec. 27, 1846; m. Dr. William H. RISK, of Summit, N. J. (deceased). 13. FRANK W., 4, b. Sept. 9, 1848; d. June 1, 1849. 14. FREDERICK W., 4, unmarried. 15. ANNA G. W., 4, b. Feb. 15, 1852; d. Nov. 4, 1853. 16. PHILEMON W., 4, b. in Newark; m., has had four children, of whom only one (XIII-4) is living. 17. WARREN W., 4, widower. 18. MARY GREEN W., 4, unmarried. 19. HENRY GREEN W., 4, b. Dec. 26, 1859; d. May 4, 1868. 20. EDMUND DRAKE W., 4, m., no children. 21. SOPHIA E. GUSTIN, 5, lived at Macon, Ga.; d. Aug. 8, 1904. 22. GEORGE WOODRUFF GUSTIN, 5, for some years a judge and member of the Georgia Senate; d. in 1895, at Macon; unmarried. 23. HELEN S. GUSTIN, 5, m. George LOGAN, of Macon, Ga. 24. WILLIAM HENRY W., 6, in Union army, killed at Gettysburg; unmarried. 25. GERTRUDE W., 6, m. James MARSHALL, of Chicago, and has two children. 26. GEORGIANA S. W., 6, is living (1905) in Minnesota; m. and with children. 27. JOSEPHINE W., 6 (deceased); m. Ralph PARKER, at Fox Lake, Wis. 28. BELLE W., 6 (deceased); m. J. M. HEWETT, of Chicago, and left three children. 29. CHARLTON DAVIS, 9; m., no children. 30. ANNA DAVIS, 9, widow of J. Lester WELLS. 31. ELIZABETH DAVIS, 9, d. when about seven years old. 32. SOPHIA E. DAVIS,

9, d. unmarried, Sept. 8, 1841. 33. ADALINE L. W., 10, m. H.
RACE, M.D., of Pittstown, N. J. 34. FRANK D. W., 10, M.D.
35. MARY EMMA W., 10, m. Rev. George W. TOMSON. 36.
HOWARD D'WOLF W., 14, graduated with highest honors from
the University of N. Y. 37. THEODORA D. W., 14, m. Thomas
W. WHITE, of the N. Y. Herald, and has children. 38. BOUGH-
TON W., 14, d. while a sophomore at the U. of N. Y. 39. ED-
WARD COURSEN W., 16, m. (1) 39 Helen Chapman, b. July 8,
1846, d. Feb. 6, 1893; m. (2) 40 Elizabeth Mills.* 41. HELEN
ELIZABETH W., 16.* 42. FRANCIS EBEN W., 16.* 43.
FREDERIC ABSALOM W., 16, m. 43 May Wilder Mills.* 44.
WILLIE AVERY WHELPLEY, 20, b. Aug. 21, 1842; d. April
20, 1844. 45. LIZZIE S. WHELPLEY, 20, b. June 20, 1856; d.
Feb. 14, 1863. 46. SARA ELIZA WHELPLEY, 20, m. William
Whelpley THOMAS. 47. EDWINA WHELPLEY, 20, b. April
18, 1845; d. Feb. 11, 1901; m. Rev. Sandford H. SMITH, w. i.
48. EDWARD WOODRUFF WHELPLEY, 20, b. Dec. 3, 1846;
d. March 4, 1887; unmarried. 49. JOANNA JOHNES WHELP-
LEY, 20; m. Eugene T. GARDNER. 50. HELEN VAN LIEU,
27; m. H. E. RICHARDS, a lawyer, of Newark, N. J. 51.
ANNA RANDOLPH, 29, m. Willard RICHARDS; has a child.
52. HUGH RANDOLPH, 29, m. and has children. 53. LAURA,
15. 54. HENRY, 15. 55. WARREN, 15.

GENERATION XIII. 1. LOUISE HARRIET SELDEN, 7, m.
Charles Sprague CAREY, of N. Y. City. 2. CLARA SAYRE
SELDEN, 7. (See also XIII-22-23.) 3. MARGARET HEN-
DERSON RISK, 12, m. Benjamin Vroom WHITE. 4. KATHA-
RINE W., 16. 5. GEORGE D. W., 17. 6. WILLIAM H. W.,
17. 7. LOUISA ADELINE LOGAN, 23. 8. GEORGIA LO-
GAN, 23. 9. HARRIET PARKER, 27. 10. CLARENCE
WELLS, 30. 11. ELSIE WELLS, 30. 12. FRANK CHAP-
MAN W., 39, b. July 15, 1867; d. Oct. 10, 1889.* 13. EDITH
WINIFRED (Daisy) W., 39, b. June 1, 1872; d. March 12, 1878.*
14. EDWARD COURSEN W., 40.* 15. MARIE ANTOINETTE
W., 40.* 16. ELISABETH W., 43,* m. Jesse Mase EDDY. 17.
WILLIAM WHELPLEY THOMAS, 46. 18. NATHALIE
AVERY THOMAS, 46. 19. ELIZABETH WHELPLEY
THOMAS, 46. 20. CHARLOTTE SYDNEY THOMAS, 46.
21. EDITH BLACHLY THOMAS, 46; m. Franklin Keith TAFT.

22. HENRY ROGERS SELDEN, 7.   23. GEORGE BALDWIN
SELDEN, Jr., 7.

AUTHORITIES.—Philemon Woodruff, Esquire; Mrs. William
Silliman, Miss Charlotte T. Woodruff, Miss Clara Sayre Selden, and
many others.

NOTE.—Generation XII, 37. Thomas Waterman White, husband of Theodora D. Woodruff, was born in New York City August 31, 1850, and died there
on December 15, 1908.

NOTES TO APPENDIX B

As stated in the Preface, this note on the writer's immediate family is added in the hope that all of the descendants of John Woodruff, 1604-1670, of Southampton, L. I., will make sure that the example is followed for their respective families; and all, at least, kept safely on record until the one comes who will precis and weave the separate notes into a Genealogy of the Long Island-New Jersey Woodruffs. It will be better if the separate notes, preferably made more comprehensive (see App. C, 2), are printed or typewritten, and sent to the New Jersey Historical Society's "Woodruff Collection" (to be), in readiness for the use of the coming genealogist.

X, 5. ABSALOM W., M.D., was b. July 1, 1791, at Pennington, N. J., but his parents quickly took him to Mendham. At nineteen he went to Succasunna, Mor. Co., and for some twenty-five years was in partnership with his eldest brother, Dr. Ebenezer Blachly W., in the Drakesville and Succasunna practice, his Succasunna home being on the Main Street, just west from the cross-road—a yellow frame house still standing, in August, 1900. On Jan. 2, 1814, he m. Eliza Drake, b. 1793 (App. D), a younger sister of the brother's wife. Mother of all his surviving children, she d. June 11, 1826. On Feb. 11, 1827, he m. (2) Elizabeth, b. Sept. 24, 1785, dau. of Preserve Riggs (Ill. G, 10), neighbor of his father at Mine Run. She d. April 18, 1828, and is bur. at Mendham. On March 22, 1831, he m. (3) Joanna Nitel Johnes, b. May 16, 1791, dau. of Dr. Timothy, and granddau. of Rev. Timothy, Johnes, of Morristown, N. J., where the husband and the first and third wives are bur. She d. Nov. 22, 1882, in her 92d year.

As told to the writer by the late Mrs. Reynolds (Martha Jane McDermott), of Brookside, who, as a girl, was a member of the doctor's household, and as confirmed by the records, in 1835 (the year the Hill Top church burned down) he had a hurry call to the Mendham practice, to take the place of the resident physician, Dr. John Wick Leddell, who retired to the Ralston homestead (next the P. O.; now occupied by Mrs. DeMott, App. E-5), at Roxiticus. Temporarily, he lived in the house at the foot of the hill (Ill. G, 5) in 1903, occupied by Assessor John Dolan; but on April 1, 1836, bought (P-3, 123) the house (Map, 7) that had been occupied by Dr. Leddell since 1803-4, just across Prospect St. from his father's former homestead (Ill. G, 6). There is a tradition that through the fault of others he lost very heavily on an investment, but otherwise he prospered. Until married, his son Eben, now an M.D., joined him in the practice; after the son's departure he took Dr. John C. Elmer into partnership. On Oct. 24, 1843, presumably no longer able to stand the fatiguing life in those days of a country doctor, he sold his practice and the house (C-4, 613) to Dr. Elmer (who afterward, in turn, sold it to the

PLATE I.—(Generation X : 5.)

late Dr. John S. Stiger, who added the rear extension to the old house, still standing in 1905). Dr. Absalom removed his household to Morristown, where his dau. Eliza and his wife's family were living. He was a ruling elder in the South Street Presbyterian Church, and continued in practice until, on March 2, 1850, after an acute illness of 48 hours (inflammation of the bowels), he d. in the 59th year of his age. An able practitioner, he was the more widely known through the medical societies. He was a mem. of the Med. Soc. of N. J., as an elected delegate from Mor. Co.; on the board of censors for Morris; the auditing committee, etc., etc. Made, on July 2, 1816, a mem. of the Morris District (now Morris Co.) Med. Society (founded June 11, 1816), he was elected its Vice-President in 1822; its President in 1824, '33, '39; its Delegate to State meetings; its Counsellor in 1837; and again in 1849, a year before his death. Deliberate and dignified, he yet had a quiet humor and kindly, helpful ways. Like his father, he is still affectionately remembered in his old homes.

XI, 16. EBENEZER BLACHLY W., 5, M.D., was b. Nov. 22, 1814, at Succasunna, where he grew up; ed. there and at the Ezra Fairchild School (147); began the study of medicine with his father, Absalom, Nov. 22, 1831 (as certified to the Mor. Co. Med. Society), and attended lectures at the College of Physicians and Surgeons, N. Y. C., during the sessions of 1833-34 (no published record for 1834-5) and 1835-36, but for family reasons did not remain to graduate. On July 17, 1836, he was licensed M.D. by the Med. Soc. of N. J., and joined his father Absalom in the Mendham practice, with promising success. On Feb. 7, 1838, he m. Elizabeth Sophia Coursen (App. D; she was b. Dec. 11, 1817, and, to the deep grief of her family, d. Jan. 21, 1881). He then entered the business establishment of his father-in-law, Abraham Coursen, in New York City, and remained there until 1845. Largely for the sake of their children, the parents removed to Morristown, N. J., and on March 31, 1845, bought (F-4, 160) from Israel, son of Caleb Russell, the house on South Street opposite the Morris Academy (now the Library and Lyceum), built, trustworthy tradition has it, shortly before the Revolution (at present, though, only the middle section remains of the original building. See "The Morris Academy").

Here they spent the rest of their lives. Welcomed as a colleague by the circle of physicians, he, however, did not practice, except in emergencies, or among those who could not pay a fee. He was one of the group who, during the great war, made sure that the wives and children of the men at the front should not suffer want. Within easy distance of the town he maintained a farm, the supervision and improvement of which brought him health as well as pleasure (the latter of the two farms thus owned, after his death was bought by John D. Canfield, Esquire, through whom it has become, as Normandie Heights, an added beauty to our town). Only once in office, when, for special reasons, he was Assessor for a term, as "one of Morristown's oldest and most respected citizens," he yet took a useful part in public affairs. He was a Trustee of the "Morristown Green," and a Director and Stockholder of the "Morris Academy," both historic associations for the public good. From May 6, 1872, a Director of the Gas Light Company (organized May 9, 1859), he was also, from July 12, 1876, annually elected its President until his death. One of the charter mems. who, in 1855, founded the Evergreen Cemetery Association, he was its Treasurer from the start until 1874, and its President from 1874 until his death, in the early morning of October 5, 1885. It was written of him, "he was a gentleman of the old school, always kind and courteous, and of fine personal presence"; "a liberal and kind-hearted neighbor, he will be greatly missed." Even to-day his children are often once more told of his kindly sympathy and help for all who needed it.

XII, 39. EDWARD COURSEN W., 16, was b. in New York City; he, on Oct. 2, 1866, m. Helen Chapman (b. July 8, 1846; d. Feb. 6, 1893). Of their two children, Frank Chapman W. was b. July 15, 1867, and d. Oct. 10, 1889; Edith Winifred (Daisy) W. was b. June 1, 1872; d. March 12, 1878. The three are buried at Morristown, N. J. He m. (2) Elizabeth Mills; their children are Edward Coursen W. and Marie Antoinette W., both under eight in 1904. When of proper age, an M. C., an old friend of the family, offered a cadetship at West Point, which he would have liked to accept, but it was thought best he should not. Instead, he was ed. at the Morris Academy and the Poughkeepsie Collegiate Institute, Prof. Bartlett. After a brief trial of business he attended medical lectures at the College of Physicians and Surgeons, N. Y. C., in 1859-60 and 1860-61; but in the latter year fell seriously ill. Then the war came. Hardly ten days up from a sick bed, he took the rating of Drum Maj. and Hosp. Steward, 2d N. J. Inf., May 2 to July 31, '61, and on July 21 was an aide on the staff of Brig.-Gen. Runyon, in the battle of First Bull Run. Oct. 31, '61, to April 26, '62, was 1st Lieut. 5th N. Y. Cav. Appointed 2d Lieut. 7th Inf. (regular army), March 24, '62; 1st Lieut., Sept. 10, '63; Capt. 12th Inf., Dec. 30, '64; Maj. 5th Inf., Jan. 2, '88; Lt.-Col. 11th Inf., April 22, '92. Retired at own request (over 30 years' service) May 4, 1892. Was many times on special duty, or holding staff positions; had nine separate commands; was in skirmish at Snicker's Gap and battles of First Bull Run, Fredericksburg, Chancellorsville and Gettysburg, being wounded in latter. Is honorably mentioned in "Records of Rebellion," Series I, Vol. XXVII, page 648. Brevetted 1st Lieut. July 2, '63; Maj., March 13, '65, "for gallant and meritorious services in the battle of Gettysburg, Pa." He has built a home for himself and his family at Glen Ridge, N. J.

XII, 41. HELEN ELIZABETH W., 16, was b. at Mendham, N. J.; ed. at Morristown schools and the Misses Green's school, N. Y. C.; lived with her parents until their deaths; except while abroad, has always made Morristown her home.

XI, 42. FRANCIS EBEN W., 16, was b. in New York City. Like his elder brother, was offered a West Point cadetship it was thought best he should not accept. Was ed. at the Morris Academy and Yale (B.A., High Oration, 1864). Just following graduation passed Maj.-Gen. Silas Casey's Board at Washington for a Second Lieutenancy, U. S. C. T.; but there were so many on the waiting list before him, that the commission did not come until after he had accepted, at the instance of President Woolsey, of Yale, a nomination by Secretary of State William H. Seward to the Imperial Maritime Customs Service of China (U. S. Dip. Cor., '64, '65).

PLATE J.—LIEUT.-COL. EDWARD C. WOODRUFF, U.S. ARMY, AND
HIS SON

On Aug. 15, 1865, he was appointed by the Inspector-General of Customs, Mr. (now Sir) Robert Hart, a Fourth Assistant. After promotions became Deputy Commissioner, 1868; Acting Commissioner, 1870; Commissioner (*i. e.*, "Collector of Customs," as we would say; relative rank, Consul), Nov., 1872; served as Commissioner at Canton and many other ports for a quarter of a century; resigned because of ill-health, March 10, 1897. Was twice Chinese Secretary to I. G.; in 1877 organized and opened the custom house at the then newly added treaty port, Wuhu; was detached on special duty in Tongking, April, June, 1885. Conferred by Imperial Decree, Civil Rank of Third Class, Feb. 3, 1878; Civil Rank of Second Class, and Double Dragon Decoration, Sept. 3, 1885. Is unmarried; has written occasional letters to newspapers, etc.; he and his sister have made a home together at Morristown.

XII, 43. FREDERIC ABSALOM W., 16, was b. at Morristown, N. J.; ed. Morris Academy and Eastman's Business College, Newark, N. J.; in his youth sought in Arizona for health; for some years took charge of his father's farm. He m. May Wilder Mills (he and his brother Edward m. sisters); dau. Elisabeth W., m. Jesse Mase Eddy; residence at Convent Station, N. J.

Authorities: Mrs. Edward W. Whelpley, Mrs. Eugene T. Gardner; Med. Soc. N. J., Dr. William T. Chandler; Mor. Co. Med. Socy., Dr. H. W. Kice; Coll. Physicians and Surgeons, Asst. Registrar E. T. Boag; Vice-Chancellor Pitney, H. C. Pitney, John D. Canfield, and many others; County Histories; Church Records; Morris Academy Minutes, etc., etc.

APPENDIX C

THE WESTFIELD WOODRUFFS

In Note 110 it is stated of Hezekiah and Mary Stites Woodruff, "For all the children, search would doubtless be rewarded with much information." Two illustrations are given below:

It is pleasant to add that Dr. A. M. Cory, of New Providence, N. J., has compiled and arranged from the original records (covering the period 1750-1835) of Rev. Jonathan Elmer, Dr. Moses Gale Elmer (his son), and Rev. Elias Riggs, an alphabetical index of baptisms, marriages and deaths (with names gleaned from church relationships and business transactions, in all 3,353 entries) of early residents of Turkey (New Providence) and vicinity. This very valuable record, it is hoped, will be published, and meanwhile information can be obtained from Dr. Cory.

*   *   *   *   *   *

WESTFIELD WOODRUFF MARRIAGES, 1759-1803.

For the following list our thanks are due to Mrs. Henry C. (H. R. C.) Cooke, of Westfield, N. J., who in May, 1902, kindly supplied it from a copy made by herself of the Westfield Presb. Church records. (See Note 107, N.B. at end.)

Of these, in a letter of Sept. 22, 1899, the then incumbent, Rev. Newton W. Cadwell, D.D., had written, "we have a perfect record since 1759"; which, on the following day, with the most courteous aid of Dr. Cadwell, the writer saw and consulted. On May 12, 1903, at Westfield, Mr. J. T. Pierson, with equal courtesy, showed the writer the records handed over to him, as representative of the Westfield church, by Dr. Cadwell, on the latter's departure to his present Atlantic City church. Mr. Pierson supposed he had a complete set of those existing, but the very valuable 1759-1803 volume was not there.

In letters of Jan. 6 and 13, 1905, Dr. Cadwell informed the writer that the record concerned "seems to be lost"; and authorized him to state "That the former Pastor, Rev. N. W. Cadwell, D.D., of Atlantic City, has an exact verbatim copy of all the records of the Westfield organization since 1759, which he expects to publish in full, when convenient, in a history of the Presbyterian Church of Westfield."

To be in readiness for the publication of this revised edition, in June, 1908, a reward of one hundred dollars was offered for the finding and restoration to the Presbyterian Church in Westfield of its missing very valuable Session Book No. 2 (1759-1803). In the Westfield *Leader* of Oct. 14, 1908, there appeared the following paragraph: "The lost Session Book has been restored to the archives of the Presbyterian Church, never to stray again, it is to be hoped."

Throughout our State there are too many other valuable old records held in trust by careless custodians, or even in the hands of those who ought to restore them to their lawful possessors. Too often, also, they are exposed to the hazard of fire, or ignorance of their value, or other cause likely to lead to their loss. In the general interests it is suggested that the State authorities initiate a concerted movement to gather all such old records in a central place of safety accessible to the public.

THE WOODRUFF MARRIAGES WERE:

Aaron,	to	Ruth Terry,	Nov. 12, 1769
Aaron,	to	Polly Clark,	Dec. 23, 1802
Abigail,	to	Wilber Clark,	Dec. 16, 1759
Asa,	to	Abigail Robinson,	Sept. 8, 1793
Betsy,	to	Thomas Baker,	Aug. 2, 1794
Cornelius,	to	Mary Osborn,	Feb. 7, 1762
Daniel,	to	Mary Pierson,	Sept. 23, 1770
David,	to	Sabora Clark,	June 11, 1765
David,	to	Hannah Smith,	Jan. 8, 1782
David,	to	Johanna Tucker,	Dec. 4, 1786
Denman,	to	Abigail Valentine,	July 12, 1791
Elias,	to	Mary Joline,	Nov. 21, 1761
Elizabeth,	to	Ebenezer Bryant,	May 9, 1759
Elizabeth,	to	Samuel Miller,	Jan. 14, 1767
Isaac,	to	Mary Little,	Nov. 19, 1761
Isaac,	to	Abigail Stites,	Nov. 12, 1766
Jemima,	to	William Baker,	June 10, 1784
Jonathan,	to	Sally Clark,	Oct. 14, 1795
Joseph,	to	Puah Ely	Jan. 17, 1762
Lewis,	to	Hannah Horton,	Jan. 19, 1785
Lydia,	to	Thomas Haviland,	Apr. 13, 1802
Mary,	to	Nathaniel Willis,	Apr. 16, 1765

Moses,	to	Phebe Woodruff,	Jan. 20, 1760
Nancy,	to	John Scudder,	Feb. 8, 1792
Nehemiah,	to	Abigail Denman,	June 4, 1769
Noah,	to	Deborah Brooks,	Jan. 6, 1767
Noah,	to	Hannah Hatfield,	May 1, 1772
Noah,	to	Polly Miller,	Oct. 5, 1794
Polly,	to	Elias Osborn,	Nov. 22, 1801
Rebecca,	to	John B. Clark,	Feb. 7, 1788
Robert,	to	Jhone High,	Mar. 4, 1781
Ruth,	to	Joseph Cory,	Mar. 1, 1799
Sarah,	to	William Clark,	Aug. 5, 1762
Sarah,	to	Joseph Denman,	June 7, 1778
Sarah,	to	Matthias Scudder,	July 17, 1785
Thomas,	to	Rebecca Merry,	Jan. 31, 1763
Thomas,	to	Sally Scudder,	Feb. 8, 1792
William,	to	Phebe Ludlum,	Jan. 27, 1803*

*"The last entry made by the Rev. Benjamin Woodruff on these church records."

TWO—HANNAH WOODRUFF WINANS' DESCENDANTS

FOR what follows we are indebted to the kindness of Professor Samuel Ross Winans, of Princeton University, who is descended (the writer has learned of him) from

[1] JOHN WINANS, d. 1694 at Elizabeth, N. J.; m. 1664, at New Haven, Susannah Melyn, b. 1643, dau. of Cornelius Melyn, patroon of Staten Island. [2] CONRAD, d. 1727-28; m. Sarah Palmer. [3] JONATHAN, 1710-74; bur. at Rahway, N. J.; m. May 4, 1731, Susannah Mills, b. Feb. 11, 1707-08; 8 children. [4] JAMES, b. Feb. 20, 1744; d. Nov. 5, 1799; of Rahway, N. J.; m. (1) Elizabeth Clawson; 3 children; (2) Elizabeth Ross, b. 1762; 6 children. [5] SAMUEL (son of James and Elizabeth Ross Winans); July 22, 1796—Feb. 22, 1887; m. (1) Amelia Zeluff, 2 children; (2) Ann Woodruff, 2 children. [6] SAMUEL ROSS, son of Samuel and Ann Woodruff Winans. [The mother was of the Elizabethtown, not Westfield, branch.] It is greatly to be desired that Professor Winans will presently give to the public the results of his study of the family history.

HANNAH WOODRUFF, as dau. of Hezekiah and Mary Stites Woodruff (Sketch IV), was of Generation IX. (See App. A.)

Born June 3, 1749; d. Oct. 29, 1833; she m. Samuel WINANS, b. March 20, 1746, d. May 6, 1830; who was a son of [3] Jonathan Winans above, great-grandfather of Professor Winans. In 1807 they moved to Miami Co., Ohio, and took up Government land. Their children were:

GENERATION X. [1] CARMAN, b. March 15, 1772; moved to Ohio; m. Susan Harris, first cousin; 4 children. [2] STE-PHEN, March 26, 1774—June 11, 1850; moved to Ohio; m. (1) Lottie Marsh, second cousin; (2) Susan ———, d. 1846; (3) Hannah Anderson, wid. of Anthony Winans, d. 1843. [3] SAMUEL, b. March 12, 1776; ran away to sea and never heard of. [4] JONA-THAN, b. Mar. 11, 1778; moved to N. Y. City; m. Susan Winans, first cousin. [5] RICHARD, Jan. 3, 1781—Jan. 12, 1863; moved to Ohio; m. Sarah Winans, first cousin, May 23, 1788—Aug. 26, 1858. [6] MARY, b. Mar. 16, 1783; m. John WINANS, first cousin, d. 1806, aged 37; in 1807 was taken by parents to Miami Co., Ohio. [7] SUSANNAH, b. Nov. 15, 1786, no record. [8] SARAH, Oct. 26, 1788—Dec. 3, 1843; m. Rev. David CLARK, first cousin, b. Aug. 28, 1776, d. Jan. 6, 1847; bur. in Mt. Pulaski, Ill. [9] FRANCES, Nov. 15, 1791—Dec. 11, 1885; m. Christly STATTLER, d. 1840, Ohio; had 13 children.

GENERATION XI. [1] SAMUEL, 2. [2] WILLIAM, 2. [3] BETSEY, 2. [4] FRAZIER (the youngest) and others, 2. [5] DAVID CLARK, 5, b. March 11, 1808; d. 1855, in California; m. Amy Rollins Winans (distant cousin), 1811-57. [6] JAMES, 5, b. May 28, 1810; d. in California; m. ——— Bailey. [7] FANNY ELIZA, 5, b. May 25, 1812; m. (probably) ——— TODD. [8] JOHN CLAWSON, 5, March, 1822-91; m. about 1870, ——— Maxwell, a wid. [9] HANNAH WOODRUFF, 5, Oct. 24, 1831-1859. [10] JOHN CLAWSON, 6, Aug. 29, 1803-1862; in 1807 taken by parents to Ohio; m. Mary Clark; was "Colonel John Wi-nans," "Judge"; had many children. [11] SAMUEL, 6; Nov. 21, 1805—Feb. 29, 1872; m. Sept. 26, 1833, Phebe Ayres; 6 children. [12] RICHARD, 8 (Rev'd; Meth.); m. Margaret Clark, first cousin; 8 children. [13] JOHN, 8, M.D., 1810-77; m. Eliza Tre-maine; no children. [14] HANNAH, 8, d. in infancy. [15] CARMAN, 8, b. 1815; m. 1836, Harriet Crocker, b. 1817; had 7 children. [16] SARAH H., 8, b. 1817; m. 1834, John RIDDLE, of Illinois; 4 children. [17] ELIZABETH, 8, b. 1820; m. 1846, Alfred GIDEON; has one son.

GENERATION XII. [1] RICHARD, 5, M.D.; 1829-82, of Benton Harbor, Mich.; m. (1) 1852, Mary Isabel Swords, d. 1861; 3 children; m. (2) 1863, Sarah Atkinson; 2 children. [2] SARAH E., 5; 1832-59; m. Lewis CORY, of California; 3 children. [3] MARY A., 5; b. 1836; m. 1855, James S. CLARK; had children. [4] JAMES L., 5; b. 1838; of California; m. 1861, Mary A. Johnson; son, Lewis F., and probably other children. [5] RICHARD M., 8; m., and has children.

Details of recent descendants are obtainable through Professor Winans.

APPENDIX D

MATERIAL ANCESTORS

THE object of these notes is to trace our own direct line, so, although collaterals are given in part, their adequate presentation is left a task for descendants in the male lines concerned. The maiden names of the wives of our ancestors have not been found in the generations (App. A), I, Thomas; II, William; V, John; and VII, Joseph.

BLACHLY

[Mary Blachly, wife of Dr. H. S. Woodruff, Generation IX, was a dau. of 5, Dr. E. Blachly, III.]

In Colonial times the spelling was "Blatchley," "Blatchly," "Blachly." Henry Barber, in "British Family Names," states that "Blatchley" was derived from the village of "Bletchley," in the north of Shropshire (Salop), England, a county on the border of Wales, whence it is reputed came

[1] THOMAS, the Immigrant; b. 1615, in England; sailed, 1635, in "Hopewell," from London; 1640, in Hartford; 1643, New Haven; 1645, Branford, Conn.; where, and in Guilford, he lived as a planter, excepting for a short stay, 1666, at Newark, N. J. In 1669 he was elected one of the Branford-New Haven boundary commissioners; 1669-70, was a Deputy at the General Court (Hartford), which, in 1670, granted him 60 acres of land. In 1674 he d. at Boston, probably while on a visit. Of his four children by his wife Susannah,

[2] AARON, b. 1644; m. Feb., 1665 (1) Mary, dau. of Robert (or Daniel) Dodd, and (2), after 1686, Sarah (or Hannah), widow of Robert Foote. Of the ten children (all by first wife),

89

[3]   EBENEZER, I, M.D., b. 1677; lived at Dix Hill, Huntington, Suffolk Co., L. I. Of his six children,

[4]   EBENEZER, II, M.D., b. at Dix Hill, Oct. 9, 1709; became a resident of Morris Co., N. J.; d. at The Ponds, near Pompton; m. (1) Hannah Miller, (2) Mary Miller. (3) Mrs. Francis, (4) Miss Estill, (5) Miss Nichols. Of his eight children,

[5]   EBENEZER, III, M,D., b. Feb. 13, 1735; m. June 19, 1758, Mary, dau. of Henry Wick (see Wick and Cooper); lived at Mendham, N. J. (Notes 140, 1; Map, 3); and by his tombstone there, d. April 19, 1805. He was one of the founders, in 1766, of the New Jersey Medical Society, and a widely known physician. (See Sketch V.) His children were:

[6]   MARY, b. March 7, 1750 (Note 117); m. May 11, 1776, Dr. Hezekiah Stites WOODRUFF (Sketch V), and d. between Dec. 13, 1822 (when she joined her husband in executing a Morris Co. deed) and 1826 (when Elizabeth Dufford became his second wife). She was, no doubt, buried in the Mendham Hill-Top graveyard, across the street from which she had been living, but her tombstone has not been found. EBENEZER, IV, M.D.; Dec. 26, 1760—Aug. 20, 1812 (Notes, 121, 139); m. Elizabeth (May 5, 1761—April 15, 1839), dau. of Col. Oliver Spencer. HENRY WICK, M.D.; 1763-1813 (Sketch V). ABSALOM, M.D.; 1765-1834 (*ibid.*). WILLIAM, M.D.; 1767-91. DANIEL, b. 1769. NATHAN, b. 1771. CORNELIUS CAMDEN, M.D., b. 1773. HANNAH, b. 1774. JUDITH, b. 1776. PHEBE, b. 1777. TEMPERANCE, b. 1780.

[7]   For the children of Mary Blachly Woodruff, see App. B. Among the children (see Hist. Bergen Co.) of Dr. Ebenezer Blachly IV was JOSEPH WARREN, Aug. 7, 1797—July 27, 1868; m. (1) Sept. 26, 1822, Caroline Wickham Tuttle (Dec. 22, 1802—July 6, 1823); (2) April 30, 1828, Mary Cooper Tuttle (March 17, 1790—Dec. 11, 1871), both daus. of Captain William and Tempe Wick Tuttle (see Wick). The only child of Joseph and Mary was

[8]   JOSEPH WARREN, II; Oct. 19, 1831—April 6, 1860; m. Dec. 11, 1856, Jane Tweedy Wilmot, b. Aug. 14, 1835; d. in Paris, Feb. 22, 1876. Their only child was

[9]   MARY LOUISA; m. Judge Enoch KNIGHT (deceased).

In learning our descent, the writer has had most essential aid

from Charles G. Blatchley, Esquire, of Philadelphia. He comes,
as we do, from (1) Thomas, 1615-74; but through (2) Moses
(brother of our Aaron), 1650-93; (3) Joshua, 1692-1742; (4)
Moses, 1722-91; (5) Aaron, 1750-1826; (6) Martin, 1770-1847;
(7) Gilbert; to (8) Charles G., who, it is earnestly to be hoped, will
some day give us the published result of his extensive researches.
Other

Authorities are Mrs. Enoch Knight; Conger's Genealogies in
Newark; Bergen and Morris Co. Hist.; Register, etc., etc., etc.

CARTRIGHT

ELIZABETH CARTRIGHT in 1601 became the wife of
JOHN WOODROFFE, 1574-1611 (Gen. IV, see App. A); in 1604
the mother of our immigrant ancestor JOHN WOODRUFFE
(Sketch II); and when widowed, the wife of Mr. John Gosmer
(Sketch I). As yet, nothing has been learned of her ancestry.

Authority: The Rev. C. E. Woodruff; Notes 5 and 13.

COOPER (CHESTER, N. J.)

[Mary Blachly, wife of Dr. H. S. Woodruff, Sketch V, was a
granddau. of 5, Mary Cooper, wife of Henry Wick, q. v., through
their dau. Mary, wife of Dr. E. Blachly, q. v.]

[1]   JOHN; 1574-1692; of Olney, in Buckinghamshire; in 1635
      came in the "Hopewell" with w. Wibroe and 4 children;
      Dec. 6, 1636, made freeman (voter) at Boston, Mass., elder
      Lynn church on organization, and in 1638 owned land there;
      1639 was one of "undertakers" of proposed settlement,
      Southampton, L. I.; in 1640 a signer of its Indian Deed
      (Sketch I). From the So. Town Records he seems to have
      been a much respected but very strenuous citizen, quite often
      in hot water, but always coming well out of it. His son

[2]   JOHN, 1625-1677, was like his father, only more so. It was
      doubtless this John Cooper who, in 1673, visiting Southold,
      when Dutch emissaries from just recaptured New York were
      there, demanding an oath of allegiance from the people of
      Suffolk Co., warned them to "take care that you come not
      with that Flag within range of shot of our village" (South-

ampton); and they decided that it would "do more harm than good" to go. He left a wid., Sarah, and three sons, of whom

[3] JAMES, d. about 1722; was a Town Trustee in 1712; and as "Justice James Cooper," which he continued to be for life, was elected on the Committee "To Enquire into ye rights of ffifteys" (Notes 70, 71 and text). Among his children was

[4] NATHAN, I, b. before 1700; m. Mary Miller, of Easthampton; about 1740 removed to Chester (then Roxbury) to., N. J.; d. bet. July 12 and Aug. 7, 1788; was bur. on the Henry Cooper farm (see 6, Henry II). He is still well remembered as a man of force, cast in the mould of his strenuous forbears. It is often told that once, when he was sure all the other church members were in the wrong, and the sorely tried parson prayed before the congregation that the Lord in His goodness might remove the cause of discord to a better world, the old gentleman shouted back, "I won't go!" and his phrase still serves locally as a handy reminder in cases of extreme obstinacy. Of his children,

[5] MARY, b. April 4, 1718; m. Feb. 12, 1735, Henry WICK, q. v.; d. and was bur. at Mendham, July 7, 1787. Having predeceased her father, she was not named in his will (T. 31-179), but her descent is proved by an item in the diary of her son-in-law and co-executor of her husband's estate, Dr. William Leddell (App. E), viz.: "1783. To sundry services in a trial with Grandfather Cooper" (i. e. "Grandfather" of his wife—Mary's dau.—Phebe); coupled with the March, 1783, and later Mor. Co. Court records of the trial, "Nathan Cooper vs. Executors of Henry Wick." That is, Mary's father was a "Nathan Cooper," and Nathan I was the only "Nathan" old enough so to have been. Moreover, in the same March term there was a separate suit of "Nathan Cooper, Jr., and Nathan Cooper, 3rd, vs. James Cooper," showing that the "Nathan" without the "Jr." or "3rd" meant Nathan I. NATHAN II (i. e. Jr.), b. March 7, 1725; m. 1748, Mehetable Seward; d. (Will; T, 37-470) Dec. 10, 1797. He was wealthy (his inventory included eight slaves, an unusual number) and a man of note. HENRY I; b. Oct. 29, 1733; m. (1) 1752, Barbara Dickason (b. 1734); (2) 1801, Mary Boyd (b. 1764); d. March

16, 1819. JAMES DAVENPORT. MARTHA JANE
(in copy of will written "Mary" in error); m. Peter CLO-
VER. HANNAH, m. ——— SATTERLY.

[6] For Mary's descendants see Sketch V; App. B and Note;
Blachly; Wick. The children of Nathan II were NATHAN
III; m. Elizabeth, dau. of Samuel Wills; d. 1834, w. i.,
their one child, a little girl, having predeceased him. ABRA-
HAM, Feb. 18, 1762—Sept. 13, 1818; m. 1799, Anna Wills
(sister of above). SAMUEL. Of Henry I; MARTHA, b.
April 21, 1756; m. ——— KELSEY. HENRY II; July
14, 1767—Feb. 27, 1825; m. Rachel, dau. of Stephen
Thompson. He built the brick (bricks stamped H. C.) house
now owned and occupied by the Romeo Robinsons, on the
road between Mendham and Chester, about a mile eastward
from the Nathan Cooper homestead. MARY, b. June 9,
1769; m. ——— MESLAR. ELIZABETH, b. Jan. 26,
1776; m. ——— WYCOFF. Of Martha Jane Clover,
LEWIS PETER CLOVER, b. Dec. 16, 1790.

[7] The children of ABRAHAM were BEULAH A., NATHAN
A. (IV); April 20, 1802—July 27, 1879; m. Mary Henri-
etta (b. July 26, 1822, dau. of Dr. John Wick and Jemima
Wills, sister of above, Leddell, q. v.). He was a Brig.-Gen.
N. J. Cavalry, and well known as a public man. Some of
his children still live at the old mansion referred to in (6).
Of Henry II, LUCETTA, 1793-1877; m. 1818, Mahlon
PITNEY (Aug., 1795—April 3, 1863). JANE, m.
Charles CONKLIN. NANCY, m. ——— GASTON.
PHEBE ANN, m. ——— ELDREDGE. MARY, m.
——— SIMPSON. LYDIA. DAVID. WILLIAM.
JOSEPH. AARON. Of Lewis Peter Clover, WILLIAM
C., b. Aug. 14, 1817 (happily still living in 1904). Rev.
LEWIS PETER, D.D. Judge HENRY ASHLEY (St.
Louis). MARTHA JANE, m. ——— TODD. SARAH
LOUISE, m. ——— POTTER; and three others.

[8] For children of Gen. Nathan A. (IV) see App. E (5). Of
the children of Lucetta Pitney, Vice-Chancellor HENRY
COOPER PITNEY, m. April 7, 1853, Sarah L. Halsted,
1828—May 28, 1899. Among the grandchildren of Lewis
Peter Clover are Capt. RICHARDSON CLOVER, U. S.
Navy; Rev. GEORGE F. CLOVER (St. Luke's Hospital,
N. Y. C.), son of Rev. Lewis P. Clover, D.D.; Prof.

HENRY A. TODD (Columbia University, N. Y. C.); and ASHLEY COOPER CLOVER (St. Louis).

[9]	The children of Vice-Chancellor Pitney are: SARAH HAL-STED; m. Finley A. JOHNSON. HENRY COOPER; m. Laura G. P. Wood. MAHLON; m. Florence Theodora Shelton. JOHN OLIVER HALSTED; m. Anne Roberta Ballentine. CATHARINE JAMES; m. George Richstein VAN DUSEN. MARY BRAYTON. FREDERICK VERNON; m. Elizabeth Willard Chadwell.

Authorities: Mrs. C. C. Davis, Miss M. E. Leddell, Vice-Chancellor Pitney, H. C. Pitney, Jr., Mr. William C., Rev. G. F. and Mr. A. C. Clover, Prof. Todd, and many others.

S. T. R. W. S. P.; Howell; County Histories, etc.

THE COURSENS
OF SUSSEX COUNTY, NEW JERSEY

THE COURSENS
OF SUSSEX COUNTY, NEW JERSEY

ELIZABETH SOPHIA COURSEN, wife of Dr. E. B. Woodruff, Gen. XI, 16, App. B and Note, was a daughter of (6) Abraham Coursen.

THERE is a widespread tradition among both the Sussex "Coursens" and the Staten Island "Corsons" that their respective ancestors were refugees from France,[1] coming, presumably, like most such refugees, by way of Holland. Toward this origin the writer, with aid, has traced the lineage of our Sussex family from the already known John Coursen (died 1770) upward three more generations. In the course of his researches he has found indications (similarity of recurring given names in the early generations of the above two families, etc., etc.)—but they may be mere coincidences—that we "Coursens," like the "Corsons," are descended from the "Vrooms"[2] of Holland. As "Vroom," or "Vroome," or "de Vroome," or "der Fromme" (meaning, in Dutch, "Pious," "the Pious") is apparently a nickname Hollanders have attached to an adult, it may have taken the place of the rightful surname, perhaps Coursen, of a French refugee. More than two years' correspondence with genealogists of standing in Holland, however, has made it evident that to test the truth of these (and other) possibilities of our lineage some enthusiastic Coursen descendant, "charged with knowledge" of the history of the American families, must make search in person in Holland.[3] This is not practicable for the writer, and at his age it would not be right to longer hold back the publication of this book for the chance of result from the work of others.

Our family owes Mr. A. J. F. van Laer, Archivist of the New York State Library, a debt of gratitude for much very kind and very efficient aid. Among many other things, he has carried us up from John Coursen (1649-1703) to his father.

1. CHRISTIAEN JANSS (Christian, son of JAN ——;

WHAT IS THE SURNAME?), of Recife, Brazil, S. A. (Recife then being in the possession of Holland). Christiaen and Janneken (Jane) Christiaens, his wife, are recorded on Aug. 1, 1649, as parents, at the baptism of Johannes,[4] known to be our ancestor.

2. JOHN COURSEN, I,[5] thus baptized[6] Johannes at Recife,[4] on Aug. 1, 1649, on Oct. 25, 1673, as Ian Corszen, of Recife, was married[7] in New Amsterdam, to Metje (Mathilde) Theunis (i. e., daughter of Theunis equals Anthonis, Anthony) Cräy.[8] In 1674, being then twenty-five years of age, he was acting as steward for the Burgomaster in issuing the garrison's provisions,[9] and is mentioned in lawsuits and otherwise. At that time his home was in the part of Beaver Street between William and Broad, once called Smith Street Lane.[10]

On July 15th of that year their first child, Margrietie, was baptized,[11] a witness being Theunis Craey,[8] and on May 10, 1676, a son Kors (Christian or Cornelius), witnesses Jan de Vries and Trijn (Catharine) van Campen, wife of Theunis Craey. There followed, on Jan. 9, 1678, a Tryntie, witnesses Hendrick Jilliszen and Marritie (Mary) van Hoboken; and on Aug. 12, 1682, Geertruyd, a witness being Grietie Hendrix. Then, until 1690, no baptisms have been found on record.

In 1686, Metje Theunis, wife of Jan Corsen, was recorded as a member of the R. D. Church, residing on the west side of Broad Street.[12] On Dec. 13th of that year John bought,[13] for "a valuable sum of money," a property on the west side of the "Sheep Pasture," south of Wall Street. In the deed he is described as a "marriner"; considering the "valuable sum of money," presumably "master marriner."

On April 6, 1690, JACOBUS was baptized; parents, Jan Corszen and Metje Cräy; witnesses, Theunis de Key and Catherina der Val; and on Sept. 2, 1692, Benjamin; witnesses, Gov. Benjamin Fletcher and wife. April 3, 1695, John Corsen, "marriner," and Metje, his wife, sold[14] their home beside the "Sheep Pasture"; of their further residences no record has been found. On July 14th of the same year came the last of the baptisms, Elisabeth; witnesses, Johannes Hardenbroeck and Margarete Meynders, wife of Colonel Ludowyc. On Feb. 29, 1696, and May 22, 1698, the wife, Metje Cray, as witness at baptisms, again appears without her husband; but on Oct. 20, 1701, they were together, when, as Jan and Mettine (clerical error?) Corsen, they indentured[15] their son Jacob to William Bogaert, Turner, of their city.

Because of intervals, as shown above, when our mariner, of whom we know so little, was apparently away from home, it is uncertain whether the absence of his name from the N. A. Census of 1703[16] means that he was on a voyage or that he had died. No later mention of him or of his wife has been found; and of his children, other than our ancestor Jacob, while there are names in the records that suggest possibilities, nothing is certainly known.

3. JACOB COURSEN, I,[17] was baptized (Jacobus) on April 6, 1690, in the Reformed Dutch Church of New York City. On Oct. 20, 1701, when he was some eleven years old, his parents, Jan and Mettine (Metje) Corsen, indentured him for six years, with provision for his education, to William Bogaert, Turner, of the same city; and on April 20, 1702, he acknowledged and approved.[15]

When, on April 3, 1717, Jacob and his wife, Adriaentje Koevert,[18] had their first-born child, the founder of our family in Sussex County, baptized John (Johannes), they were members[19] of the Church of the River and Lawrence Brook, a branch of the Raritan (Somerville) Church, at Six Mile Run,[20] near New Brunswick; and were living at or near Neshanic,[21] in the now Hillsborough township of Somerset County. There followed baptisms at Six Mile Run of Jannike (Jane), March 27, 1820; Metje (Mathilde), March 11, 1722; Margrietje, December 20, 1724; Teunis (Anthony), July 23, 1727.

After the latter date Jacob removed his family just across the county line into Readington township, Hunterdon County; the Readington church records[22] showing the baptism there of their daughter Geertrug (Gertrude) on May 11, 1732. Here he probably owned, and lived near by, the mill on the South Branch of the Raritan River, beside the road (then crossing the Branch a little lower downstream than now), between Flemington and the hamlet of Barley Sheaf.[23] The surrounding country was very pleasing to the eye, and there were friendly neighbors: Gov. John Reading,[24] Abraham Zutphen, John Aller, witnesses to his will; his son-in-law, Benjamin Cole; Martin Ryerson, and other well-known names. On Holland's Brook, near Readington village, were Douwe and Benjamin Corsen, from Staten Island.[25]

Of his immediate family, John had struck out for himself and gone into Morris County; Jane, after becoming Mrs. David McKenney, had died, leaving a daughter Ida; Mette (Matte) was unmarried; Margaret was Mrs. James Smock; Teunis (Tunis) had a wife Hannah and twins, Mally and Metje; Gertrude was Mrs. Benjamin Cole. His pleasant surroundings could not be enjoyed forever. On March 12, 1756, "being sick and weak in body," he made his will,[26] and before the third day of July following he died, in the sixty-sixth year of his age.

4. JOHN COURSEN, II, son of Jacob and Arryante Corson, was baptized Johannes, on April 3, 1717 (Somerville-Raritan records, 1717-27). His parents were then living in Somerset Co., N. J., but before 1732 were residents of Readington to., Hunterdon Co., where, on Aug. 14, 1743,[27] Jan Korsen and his wife, Geertje,[28] had a son Jacob baptized, and on June 23, 1745, a son Isaac.[29] No further record has been found of him until, among the papers filed with his father Jacob's original will,[26] his administrator's bond shows that on Aug. 20, 1756, he was of Roxbury to., Morris Co., N. J.[30]

He next appears in Sussex Co., N. J., where, on May 14, 1763,[31] he bought from Joseph Hull, of New London, Connecticut, a tract of about 850 acres,[32] and another of 806 acres,[33] in Hardwicke (now Stillwater) to., at Coursen's Corners (now Fredon), some four miles south of west from Newton, the county seat. On the same day he executed a mortgage to Mr. Hull on 750 of the acres,[34] pledging the payment money on or before Aug. 1, 1764. Two days later Mr. Hull, at New London, gave a power of attorney[35] for all his remaining New Jersey lands to his "Trusty and well-beloved friend Mr. John Corson of Hardwick," etc., etc. On July 12, 1764, just before the above payment money would fall due, John Corson sold to John Roy, Esquire, of Bernard's Town,[36] Somerset Co., 220 acres, being part of the 806 acres tract.[33]

The wife who joined him in executing this conveyance was named Charity; so the wife of his youth, Gertrude van Tuyle,[28] had died.[37] As shown by his will,[38] made when "very sick and weak in body," John Corson[39] himself died in January-February, 1770. While from the extensive real estate transactions, and from the wording of Mr. Hull's power of attorney, he was evidently a man of means and of standing, from his death, at the early age of fifty-three, and from the need of the gallant and successful struggle of the son who followed him as the head of the household, it is possible that he suffered from the then common fault of buying too much land for his strength. The two elder sons having apparently set up for themselves, and Benjamin, who sold part of his inherited lands, perhaps not being helpful, the care of the bereaved mother and younger children fell on the next in order of age,

5. JOHN, III. Born Sept. 7, 1753, he was thus but a strip-

ling of hardly seventeen, yet gradually bought all the lands sold by Benjamin; served in the Revolution as Sergeant, then Ensign in the Second Regt. Sussex Militia (Stryker); June 5, 1793 (as known to us through the courtesy of Adjutant-General, Trenton), was commissioned Major, Sussex Militia; March 10, 1798, Lt.-Colonel 4th Sussex Militia; and in 1805 replaced the first log-house with the very attractive homestead still standing in its garden on the knoll. He was an ancestor to be proud of! He d. Jan. 12, 1815, and is bur. in the old Hardwicke (now called "Yellow-frame," *i. e.,* yellow-painted frame church) graveyard, 3½ miles west of south from the homestead, as are many of his descendants. In 1779 he had m. Phœbe Goble (Sept. 21, 1760—March 22, 1819). Their children were:

6. ENOS, Oct. 19, 1780—Oct. 17, 1819; m. Mary Green (1785-1863); lived at the homestead. ABRAHAM, July 10, 1784 —Jan. 17, 1843; m. Sept. 23, 1813, Mehitabel (Hetty) Marsh, q. v.; of Washington Square, N. Y. C.; merchant. ANN, Dec. 22, 1787—April 28, 1872; m. Abram BUNTING (d. 1851). ISAAC VANTILE, July 10, 1794—Aug. 4, 1855; m. Phebe Hurd (Aug. 4, 1800—April 23, 1885); lived at homestead. GERSHOM, June 5, 1795—May 19, 1821. SARAH, May 25, 1797-1852; m. 1821, Richard STILLWELL (d. 1861).

7. Among the children of Enos were AARON, 1808—Aug. 29, 1828; bur. Hardwicke graveyard. GERSHOM HAMPTON, 1810 —Jan. 22, 1886; m. (1) Susan Paul; (2) 1845, Caroline Higbie (1822—May 10, 1883); of New York City. Of Abraham: ELIZABETH SOPHIA, m. Dr. E. B. WOODRUFF (App. B and Note). WILLIAM A., Nov. 21, 1819—Sept. 16, 1895; m. (1) Sophia C. Raphael (1821-43); (2) Henrietta M. Oakley (1820-49); (3) Jane Chester. He was a graduate of the University of the City of New York, and a lawyer in that city. It was written of him: "He stood high among his associates in the law"; "as the Mayor of Elizabeth he made an enviable record"; "he was twice elected . . . each time by heavy majorities"; "his terms of office have often been cited as models"; "he was one of the most respected citizens of the State." SARAH ANNA, Feb. 23, 1822—Aug. 15, 1868; unmarried. ISAAC OLIVER, M.D., Feb. 9, 1829—March 31, 1873; m. Virginia Calhoun; d. Aug. 20, 1906. Isaac Vantile's children: JOHN ABRAHAM, June 27, 1819—July 8, 1837. JOSEPH H., b. June 4, 1821 (deceased). GERSHOM A. S. WHITEFIELD. L. OSCAR, living at homestead. HAMPTON A., mer-

chant, N. Y. C., living at East Orange, N. J.; m. Sarah E. Stillwell (1832-1901). LOUISA E., b. Nov. 22, 1829 (deceased). Hon. WILLIAM P., mem. N. J. Legislature, 1894-96; living at homestead; m. Emma C. Coursen (July 19, 1837—June 1, 1877). S. AMANDA, m. ——— MANNING. ADDIE N., b. Feb. 13, 1835 (deceased). EDGAR A., b. June 8, 1837 (deceased). ISAAC VANTILE, b. Aug. 26, 1839 (deceased). Col. HENRY A., of Scranton, Pa.; Sec. Lieut. Oct. 3, 1861, First Lieut. Sept. 5, 1862, 7th N. J. Inf.; Capt. March 22, 1863, 23d N. J. Inf. The children of Sarah Stillwell: WILLIAM E., 1822-80. JOHN OSCAR, 1826-58. RICHARD H. SARAH E., 1832-1901; m. Hampton A. COURSEN.

8. The children of Gershom Hampton and Susan Paul: PAULINE, m. Henry S. OSBORN; of G. H. and Caroline Higbie, GEORGE HAMPTON, m. Charlotte Potter Higginson (d. Oct., 1891). CHARLES, d. in infancy. CHARLOTTE HIGBIE. MARY, d. 1865. ROBERT LEWIS. For the children of Elizabeth Sophia Woodruff, see Note to App. B. Of William A. and Sophia Raphael, ANNA RAPHAEL, June 25, 1840—March 4, 1877. Of William and Henrietta Oakley, HENRY DEE, Sept. 1, 1845—Oct. 17, 1866. WILLIAM A., JR., d. aged 6 mos. 2 days. HENRIETTA OAKLEY, m. Herbert B. ROBESON (Oct. 20, 1847—Nov. 23, 1906). Of William and Jane Chester, FRANCES BELL. ALFRED CHESTER, m. Sophia Johns. EDITH C., m. Edward P. THOMPSON. WILLIAM A., m. Harriet Van Wyck Bennett. JANE C., m. Howard C. LEVIS. Of Isaac Oliver, FLORENCE LESLIE; Nov. 12, 1858—Oct. 11, 1862. VIRGINIA, m. Noble C. WILLIAMS; d. June 5, 1906. LUCY (deceased), m. Col. James T. WRIGHT. BERTHA L., m. Col. James T. WRIGHT. Of Hampton A., ELLA S. FRANK E., m. Jessie E. Vilas. Of Hon. William P., MARIETTA; d. March 12, 1875, aged 5 mos. 19 days. FRED W., m. Ella M. Johnson. NELLIE L., m. Hampton ROY; three children.

The best authority on the Sussex Coursens is Mr. Jacob Allen Coursen, of Branchville, N. J. His own lineage is: Jacob, son of John II; July 30, 1743—Jan. 5, 1815; m. Mary Nixon (Aug. 9, 1742—April 12, 1828). Allen, Dec. 3, 1772—July 12, 1816; m. Nov. 4, 1807, Charity Cummins (d. May 30, 1817). William Nixon, b. July 12, 1811. Jacob A., who, it is hoped, will publish the results of his successful labors.

Authorities: Miss Charlotte H., Miss Ella S., Messrs. Jacob A.,

William P. and Henry A. Coursen. Bergen's King's County, N. Y. (Vroom), and Hist. Bergen Family (p. 128). Weiss, Hist. French Huguenots. Fernow's N. A. Family Names and their Origin; Half-moon Series, Vol. II, No. 6 (pp. 213-16). Aliases of Males, Ref. Dutch Ch., 1636-1756, in Holland Society Year Book, 1896 (pp. 190-98). Clute, S. I. Morris, S. I. Hist. City of N. Y., Mrs. Martha J. Lamb. N. J. Archives, Vol. XXI, First Series. County Hists. Descendants Benjamin Corson, etc., etc., etc.

NOTE.—Generation 7, pp. 101-2. Hampton Aaron Coursen, born July 12, 1827, died at East Orange, N. J., on Dec. 19, 1908.

NOTES ON THE COURSENS

Abbreviations

A. N. F.; Algemeen Nederlandsch Famlieblad (periodical; bound volumes at N. Y. H. S. and Astor Library, N. Y. C.). *G and B.;* New York Genealogical and Biographical Record. *H. S. Y. B.;* Holland Society Year Book. *N. A.;* New Amsterdam. *N. J. A.,* New Jersey Archives. *N. Y. H. S.;* New York Historical Society. *N. Y. S. O.;* New York Surrogate's Office. *R. D.;* Reformed Dutch. *S.;* Sussex County, N. J. *T.;* Trenton, N. J.

Genealogical Data

CORSON (Staten Island, etc.); *Notes* 1, 2, 25, 30. COURSEN (Sussex Co.); 1, 4, 23, 30, 37, 38. SPELLING OF DITTO: 1, 17, 21, 39. CRAEY, de CROY; 8. KOEVERT; 18. LAKER-MAN; 28. READING; 24. VAN TUYLE; 28, 30. VROOM; 2, 4, 30.

1. FRENCH COURSENS. In her delightful "Romance of a Coursen Quest" (not yet published) Miss Charlotte H. Coursen (Generation VIII) has told us that the Coursens had their origin in France, in which country was the place that gave the place-name (also written Courson, Courçon, Curson, Curzon, etc.); the belief is widespread among us. For the similar tradition among the Corsons, see "The Corson Family, A History of the Descendants of Benjamin Corson, Son of Cornelius Corssen of Staten Island, N. Y." By Hiram Corson, M.D., of Plymouth Meeting, Pa. Printed for private distribution, Philadelphia. Henry Lawrence Everett, publisher, 227 South Sixth Street. (No date.)

2. VROOM. The earliest record of Vrooms in Holland known to the writer is of the Haarlem family (see the periodical, "Oud Holland," 1900, copy at N. Y. State Library, Albany). Its founder, Hendrick, a sculptor, was the father of, among others, Cornelius, a sculptor; who was the father of, among others, Hendrick, a marine painter of note, who was born at Haarlem in 1566, and was buried there in 1640. While further search may reveal even earlier dates there, or elsewhere, yet the Vrooms might have been refugees from France, religious persecution having begun in that country still earlier, and there having been, for example, early Vrooms at Leiden, a favored resort of such refugees.

The first known Vroom in New Amsterdam, Cornelius Pietertse Vroom (as written by the historian Bergen), living when everybody there knowing everybody else, surnames were superfluous, was recorded only as "Cors Pietersz" (Cors, son of Peter); but in signatures his mark ⌐⊢— distinguished him from a contemporary "Cors Pietersz," a seaman, still living in 1661, after the former had died. That the omitted surname was "Vroom," we know from the fact that in the more sophisticated following generation his sons were so recorded.

His initial record, in 1638, referred to an inheritance by his wife, Tryntje (Catherine) Hendricks (Cal'r of Dutch MS., pp. 5, 62; N. Y. Coll. MS., Vol. I, p. 72), and showed that he was born about 1611-1612, and was from Langeraer, a hamlet northeast of Leiden; but search has failed to find any trace of him there, or in the neighborhood, or at Langerak of Schoonoven, presumably from the inadequacy of their records of that early time. He died before 1657, in which year his widow, Tryntje, when marrying Frederick Lubbersen, requested guardians for the three infant sons of "Cors Pietertse," viz., Cornelius, Pieter, and Hendrick. (Orphan Masters of N. A., pp. 37, 40; N. Y. R. D. Church Baptisms, pp. 19, 29, 36; Bkn. R. D. Church baptisms, pp. 35, 39.)

The descendants of the son Cornelius Corssen (son of Cors) Vroom, 1645-93, dropping the "Vroom" (perhaps remembering an earlier surname), became the "Corsons" of Staten Island, New Jersey (chiefly from Hunterdon County southward) and Pennsylvania. Pieter Corssen, 1651-96, or later, is supposed (Bergen's "King's County") to have had a son, Jacob Corson, who, or whose son Jacob, in 1770 left a widow, Hester, dau. of Jabez Heaton, of Mount Olive, then in Roxbury to., Morris Co., N. J. (Trenton Wills, K-256), who may have borne him children, but no trace of their descendants has been found. The third son of Cors Pietertse, Hendrick Corsen Vroom (1653—"to a good old age"), was the ancestor of the New Jersey Vrooms. There is material in the records for more detailed narratives of their lives.

3. THE HOLLAND CORRESPONDENCE began on March 31, 1906, and still continues. With a solitary disappointment (Mr. A. A. Vorsterman van Oijen) there has been very courteous willingness to aid, notably shown in the wise and friendly advice of Maj. J. G. Gysberti Hodenpijl van Hodenpijl, a retired officer of the Dutch Army, who has done much good genealogical work. To him, and to the other gentlemen who, unprofessionally or professionally, have done so much, even though unavailingly, the writer's sincere thanks are due, and are here cordially tendered.

The object of the correspondence is to connect our Coursen line with Holland (on the way to France) by finding in the records the JAN ———? (see text) who was the father of CHRISTIAEN JANSS (son of Jan), of Recife. As a beginning, attempt is being made to ascertain whether (as seems possible) this "Jan" was a "Jan Vroom." Should this fail, there would needs be a wider search for any "Jan" of any surname who so suited in dates and circumstances as evidently to have been the sought-for father. In either case, if one "Jan" is found not to suit, it is only to try another, until the records have been exhausted, and we have found or failed. As the father of a Christian who had a son baptized in 1649 would have been born in the generation before, say, 1630, and as Holland's records for such early days are but scanty, the task is by no means an impossible one. In the case of Christian's son John, it has been accomplished here where the old archives are more extensive. Moreover, experience has shown that while following the many wrong clues, one steeped in the subject may stumble across the right one.

At long range, however, the task requires too much time to be practicable. Besides the delays inevitable when letters have to cross the ocean, even eminent professional genealogists, who have not been able to make a special study of the subject, when searching the records may not see an earmark in an item that would be significant to a searcher who, although only an amateur, was charged with the particular knowledge. For example, in one long list of records supplied there was an item of the appointment, May 19, 1617, of a guardian for a child, JAN DE VROOME (and his brother and sisters). Had this Jan been born not later than, say, 1608, he might have had a son Christian born in 1628, who had our ancestor baptized in 1649; so his record had to be looked into. But after inquiry had brought out the fact that he was not born until 1610, this obviously became too improbable, so it was only to seek for another "Jan Vroom." Yet, although the age was known, and could have been stated in the item first sent, it took the writer more than three months to ascertain it; the all-importance first of the "Jan," and then of the "1610" being so late as to make further search for his history useless, not having been realized through lack of familiarity with the annals of the American Coursens.

When an enthusiastic Coursen, charged with special knowledge, can sit at the elbow of the eminent genealogist, it should be speedily determined whether or not we can trace our lineage in the records of Holland. Unhappily, wars and catastrophes have played sad havoc with the early archives of that gallant State.

4. RECIFE VROOMS (?). Recife (The Reef), Pernambuco, Brazil, S. A., from A. D. 1630 to 1654 was in the possession of Holland (see any history of Brazil). After careful search through its baptismal records (A. N. F., Vols. V, 1888, VI, 1889), Mr. A. J. F. van Laer (see text) found that the only Jan or Johannes in them, whose father's given name could possibly have caused our ancestor to be known as Ian Corszen (son of Cor—Christian or Cornelius), of Recife, is this son of Christiaen Janss.

Among the suggestions that this Christian's father, Jan, may have been a Jan Vroom are the following: There was at least one Vroom at Recife, a Hendrick (like Jan, a recurring Vroom name), who was parent at a baptism in 1639, and a witness in 1650, 1651 and 1652. In the baptismal list on the same date, and immediately following our Christian, a Frederick Janss, apparently a brother, and his wife Grietien (Margaret) had a son Jan (and a dau.) baptized. The given name, "Frederick," is an early Vroom name in Holland, while "Christian" is found in the early generations of the N. A. Vroom-Corsons; and there is further similarity of recurring names in that and our Coursen families.

5. JOHN'S SURNAME was variously spelled in the records as Corszen, Corssen, Korssen, Corsen, Coerson (H. S. Y. B., 1896, p. 174), Coursen (N. Y. Reg. Office; Deeds, 13-234).

6. A. N. F., Vols. V, 1888, VI, 1889, Recife Baptismal Records.

7. G. and B., 1902, p. 122.

8. CRAEY, Craie, Cray, Kray. The wife, Metje Theunis

(G. and B., 1902, p. 122; hereafter in this note, where not otherwise specified, the G. and B. is the authority), daughter of Teunis (Anthonis) Cray, was baptized in the R. D. Church, N. A., on June 12, 1650. While in the marriage record she was "Metje Theunis" (Metje, daughter of Theunis ————), the wife of this same John Coursen was elsewhere more often recorded "Metje Cray." That the "Metje" was "Mathilde," not as often "Margaret," seems probable, because her son Jacob (q. v.), in 1722, named one daughter Metje, perhaps after his mother, and in 1724 named the next daughter Margrietje, perhaps after an aunt (Note 4).

In his "Hist. of the Huguenots in America" (Vol. I, pp. 149, 167, 175, 352, 354) Baird tells us that—besides other French refugees from as early as 1546—immediately after the Massacre of St. Bartholomew, on Aug. 24, 1572, large numbers fled to Holland from the Walloon country, on the borders of France and Belgium. At Leiden, on April 12, 1613, and again on March 28, 1621, Jean de Croy had a child baptized in the Walloon church. In 1622 he joined with others of the Leiden refugees in a petition, later granted, to be permitted to emigrate to America; and, with a wife and five children, was one of those who had arrived in New Amsterdam as early as 1626.

Baird adds that of these were some "whose names may be recognized more or less readily in spite of the Batavian disguises in which they appear beyond the gap of fifteen or twenty years in the records of New Amsterdam. Such are the names of (many others and) de Croy."

Apparently, then, it was a de Croy who, as Theunis Cray, skipper, witnessed a baptism in 1640. The records of the time also show a presumably other de Croy in a Theunis Craey, wife Tryntje van Campen, whose multifarious activities ashore preclude the idea of a seafaring life in addition. Innes ("N. A. and Its People") writes of his busy and troubled career. He was first on record in 1639. Between 1642 and 1648 he had four children baptized, viz., Janneke, Grietie, Lysbeth, and Gerrit. The authorities having called in question his sale of a house to a Jew in 1655 (the first arrival of Jews was in 1654), on March 14, 1656, he told the Council that he was then about to sail for the Fatherland. In April, 1657, Theunis Craey, wife and four children, arrived at New Amsterdam from Venlo in Upper Gelderland. Both husband and wife had died before 1682.

The Anthonis (Teunis) Cray who had our Metje baptized in

1650, while none but this baptismal record has been found regarding him, is apparently not the same de Croy, because there were still but four children on the return from Venlo. There seems to have been still another de Croy in the Teunis Geurtzen Craey who, on March 16, 1653, had a daughter Lysbeth baptized, and in 1654 leased Long Island lands (H. S. Y. B., 1900, pp. 176, 177) from Teunis Craey. It should be noted that the baptismal dates of the children above named all fall within the brief interval between 1642 and 1653. In addition, there are other Craeys of the time on record with given names different from those already mentioned. From the number of these separate individuals apparently related other than as father and son it seems possible that more than one of the five de Croy children of 1626 left issue; but because of the gap in the records we have no means to trace from which of them we came. The most that can be hazarded as to the lineage of Mathilde, wife of John Coursen, is that she was a descendant of the Huguenot Jean de Croy.

9.   N. Y. Docy. Hist., II, 722.

10.   H. S. Y. B., 1896, 174.

11.   For record of this and following baptisms see G and B Indexes, R. D. Church of N. A.; List of Baptisms.

The witness Theunis Craey is mentioned in (8). Of the other witnesses, Bergen's "King's County" tells us that Gerret Jansen van CAMPEN bought a house and lot in Flatbush on Dec. 27, 1678. Benjamin FLETCHER was Governor of New York from Aug. 28, 1692, to 1698-99. He was a man of note, about whom much, both for and against, may be found in the histories. Johannes HARDENBROECK, wife and four children, were immigrants Jan. 20, 1664 (H. S. Y. B., 1902-27). Jan HENDRICKS was one of the first settlers in Bushwick, and a magistrate in 1663. Marritie van HOBOKEN married Jan Gillis. Hendrick JILLISZEN was a son of Gillis de Mandeville. Theunis de KEY, born in New York, married Helena van Brugge in May, 1680. Charles LUDOWICK was first captain, then colonel, of militia, and is prominently mentioned in the histories. Jan Jacob de VRIES was a resident of Brooklyn in 1667.

12.   Mem. Hist. N. Y., I, 449.

13.   N. Y. Reg'r O.; Deeds; 13-234.

14.   Albany; Deeds; 9-648.

15.   N. Y. H. S. Coll., Vol. XVIII. App., April 28, 1702. Original record in office of City Clerk, N. Y. C. As the few facts

known indicate that the parents were in good circumstances, the apprenticing is not likely to have been caused by pecuniary need. While there may have been special reasons, such as the father's intended absence on a long voyage, or failing health, it is more probable that it was simply because the times were different. Even much later budding physicians, for example, were similarly indentured: and Jacob apparently preferred "turner" to "yeoman" when presumably qualified for the latter. (See Note 23.)

16. O'Callaghan's Documentary Hist. of New York; Vol. I, p. 395.

17. G. and B., 1880, p. 140. His surname was variously written Corssen, Korssen, Corsen, Corson, Corse, Korse, Corser.

18. KOEVERT, Koevers, Coevers, Kuvers; Adriaentje (also written Arryante, etc.) was a daughter of Jan and Jane (Boka, Bragon) Koevers of Millstone, Somerset Co., N. J. (N. J. A., Vol. XXIII, p. 277.) This Jan Koevers, yeoman, who died between 1719 and 1723, was on record in Brooklyn, 1677-87, and in New Jersey as early as 1705. He was a son of Teunis Janse Koevers (or Coevers), of Brooklyn (and his wife Barbara Lucas); immigrant in 1651 from Heemstede in North Holland (Bergen's "King's County").

19. Steele's Hist. Discourse, App., pp. 178, 209; Messler's Notes, p. 208.

20. From 1872, "Franklin Park," on the joint boundary of Somerset and Middlesex Counties.

21. Snell's Hist. of Somerset Co., pp. 785, 788. The earlier Coursens, near Neshanic, spelled their name "Coerson." (See Note 5.)

22. Original Baptismal Record of the Readington R. D. Church; once the "North Branch" division of the Raritan (Somerville) Church.

23. The first clue to the previously unknown, but now proven by the records, parentage of John Coursen II, 1717-1770, was found among papers (with Col. H. A. Coursen, of Scranton, Pa.) left by him as administrator of his father Jacob's estate, in a deed of Dec. 21, 1755, in which John Reading, yeoman, of Amwell to., Hun. Co., conveyed to Jacob Corsen, turner, of Reading to., Hun. Co., 3¾ acres of "3d dividend" land in the latter township, having as its northwesterly boundary the "King's Road." The "3d dividend," "Reading to.," and "King's Road," taken together, limit the locality to the southerly side of the road leading from Flemington to Barley

Sheaf, easterly of the South Branch of the Raritan, which that road then crossed a little lower downstream than now. Diligent search has made it seem probable that the lot has become a part of a tract of 17 85-100 acres that has been traced upward from John Voorhees (and later owners) to a conveyance, of Feb. 13, 1798, from David and Deborah Barton, or Bartron, to John Huffman (see "Assignment of Dower" to widow Rebecca Huffman; copy kindly supplied by heirs), where the records fail. This tract is near the present mill on the Branch where the Flemington road crosses it, a predecessor of which was long known as the highest upstream of John Reading's three mills, but later as Mettlar's, Stover's, and many others.

Jacob having been a resident of Reading to. since 1732, was not likely to have needed the little lot for himself; but as the elder of his two sons, John, had gone to Morris Co., might have wished it, when nearing his death, to keep his younger son, Teunis, and wife Hannah, still close to him after their first-born (twins), baptized on Aug. 10th, only a few months before, had made a separate residence for them desirable. Moreover, Jacob was a turner. His son John had an interest in the mill adjoining his Sussex property. John's son Jacob owned the mill. This Jacob's sons were able, widely known machinists and wheelwrights, building many mills. Taking it all in all, therefore, it has seemed reasonable to assume in the text that the Jacob of 1690-1756 owned, and had his homestead near by, the mill on the Branch, beside the King's Road.

24. JOHN READING was a son of John and Elizabeth Reading, of England, who, prior to 1685, settled in Gloucester, N. J., where the son was born on June 6, 1686. He was educated in England, and married Mary, daughter of Col. P. Ryerson. Beginning as a surveyor at Gloucester, he removed to the part of Amwell now Raritan to. Here he became owner of an extensive tract of land, and built himself a mansion, still standing, on a hill westward of and overlooking the Branch, near the present Chamberlin mill, a mile or so downstream from the Barley Sheaf road. He became one of the prominent men of the State: was a member of the Colonial Council from 1728, and vice-president for ten or twelve years. Upon the death of Gov. Hamilton in 1747 the government devolved upon him until the arrival of Gov. Belcher. Again, on the death of the latter official, in 1757, he became the chief magistrate of the colony until the coming of Gov. Bernard in 1758. He died Nov. 7, 1761.

25. Jacob Corssen, son of Captain Cornelis Corssen (Vroom),

both of Staten Island (Bergen's "King's County," etc., etc.), in his will (N. Y. S. O., 21-51), signed 1742, bequeathed lands in Hunterdon Co., in or near "Reding" to., that he had purchased from John Bud, to his sons Douwe and Benjamin, both of whom appear as fathers in the Readington Church records from 1740 on. In a deed of June 1, 1721 (Burlington, D-18; N. J. A., Vol. XXI), John Budd, of Philadelphia, conveyed to Jacob Corssen, of Staten Island, 525 acres in Hunterdon Co., "near a branch of Raritan river, called Hollan's Brook." Holland's Brook rises a few miles west of the village of Readington, and perhaps a mile southeast of it leaves Hunterdon Co.

26. In his will (T. 8-399; orig'l in Hunterdon files, 1753-60) he left the use for life, of both real and personal estate, to his "Loving wife Ariantz," the personal estate, after her death, to be equally divided among the heirs. To John, in addition to the share of the personal estate "in full demand of his Birthright or Primogeniture," he devised only three shillings, the amount presumably denoting that John had already received the equivalent of his share of the real estate. This was left to Teunis, on condition of a prescribed money payment to his sisters. In default, it was similarly to go to John; but if he also did not comply with the conditions, the property was to be sold and the "nett produce" equally divided among the heirs. Sons-in-law James (Jacobus) Smock and Benjamin Cole were named executors, but in view of these conditions not unnaturally declined; so John was appointed administrator.

27. Readington Church records.

28. Geertruyd van TUYLE (as spelled for a son thus named in her husband's original will) was baptized (G. and B., 1905-1906) at Port Richmond, Staten Island, on April 6, 1724; the date of her death is not known.[37] Her parents were Isaac and Sara (Lakerman) van Tuyl.

As stated in the Introduction (p. 11) to the "History of the Bergen Family," the van Tuyles (van Tuyl, van Tuil, van Thull, etc., etc.) of Holland are recorded among the armor-bearers in the "Genealogical Chart of the Netherlands Race"; and their coat-of-arms is displayed in that and similar authorities. Our immigrant ancestor is believed to have been Jan Otto van Tuyle, who, with wife and two children, came to New Amsterdam on April 16, 1663. At Port Richmond, S. I., there were the following baptisms: Oct. 2, 1705, (parent) Abraham van Tuil, (dau.) Geertruyt, who married Gerrit Croesen, (a witness being) Isaac F. van Tuil; Sept. 20, 1709, (parent) Isaac van Tuil, (dau.) Catharyntie, (witnesses) Abraham van Tuil and Maria Lakerman; May 1, 1720, (parents) Isaac and Sara van Tuyl, the parents of our Geertruyd, (dau.) Catharina, (witnesses) Abraham Lakerman and Antje van Tuyl; Jan. 2, 1734, (parent) Abraham, son of Isaac van Tuil, (son) Jan. Evidently the "Abraham" and "Isaac" came to the Coursens from the van Tuyles, and to the van Tuyles they perhaps came from

LAKERMAN (Lake, Leek, Leuck; Bergen's "King's County," p. 179). Jan Lakerman, wife Ann Spicer, was at Gravesend by or before 1656, and on its Assessment Rolls as late as 1683. Gravesend having been settled as early as 1640, by immigrants chiefly from Massachusetts (Thompson's "Long Island," II, 168, 177), Lady Moody coming in 1643 (Leslie's "Greater New York," I, 36, etc.), Jan may have been a John Lake, of English descent. Daniel Lakerman, of Gravesend, wife Elizabeth Sutvin, had removed to Staten Island before Dec. 1, 1696. ABRAHAM Lakerman, son of this Daniel, was on record at Gravesend in 1691, and from the Port Richmond baptismal list, doubtless accompanied his father to Staten Island.

29. Accidentally omitted from "A Branch of the Woodruff Stock," Part III, Appendix D.

30. In 1756 "Roxbury township" included the Chester, Washington and Mount Olive townships, and parts of the Roxbury, Mendham and Randolph townships of to-day. There are indications that John Coursen's Roxbury home was in the neighborhood of the present village of Mount Olive. First, while it may be a mere coincidence of similar surnames, there was another Corssen of that period settled there. As this Jacob Corssen (died about 1770) had a daughter "Hester" baptized on Staten Island in 1701, he may be taken as the corresponding Jacob, son or grandson of Pieter, son of Cors Pietertse Vroom of N. A.,[2] and as the husband of Hester Heaton Corsen, who was granted letters of administration (T. Wills, K-256) for his estate. Now the father-in-law named therein, Jabez Heaton, lived close to the village. Second, Abraham van Tuyle, from the given name presumably a relative of John's wife,[28] in 1790 bought (Mor. Co. Deeds, L-2, 270) lands in Roxbury, and the Van Tuyle house is still (1906) standing, two or three miles northeasterly from the village, at the place where the road from Budd's Lake to Drakesville (Ledgewood) crosses that from Flanders to Stanhope.

Whether or not John Coursen, in 1756, was living in this neighborhood could probably be decided by reference to the early records of the Mount Olive Church, founded in 1753, and it was hoped that some of them had passed with other papers to Mr. John M. D. Barnes, of Dover, N. J., as nephew of the executor of Deacon Cozad of that church; but Mr. Barnes has been unable to find in his collection anything of dates 1753-1800 that relates to Mount Olive or its church.

31. Sussex Deeds, B-275, Abraham Coursen and wife, grantors.

32. Proprietors' Grants, Burlington, M-107.

33. Proprietors' grants to Mary (Jobson) Lowell and Catherine Jobson, from whom to Joseph Hull. Burlington, B-109; EF-259. The number of acres varies in the successive surveys.

34. T. Mort., W-371. This mortgage of May 14, 1763, in which no wife joins, describes him as of Hardwicke, so he may have been living there prior to that date.

35. Original, now with Col. H. A. Coursen, of Scranton, Pa. There are other papers left by John II with him and with his brother, Hon. W. P. Coursen, of Fredon.

36. T., AK-455. The wording of this conveyance of July 12, 1764, in which a wife joins, indicates that the Bernardsville of today, known in Revolutionary times as Vealtown, was then called Bernard's Town.

37. As no wife joined John in executing the mortgage of May 14, 1763,[34] apparently Gertrude had died prior to, and Charity was married later than, that date; but the latter had become the second (so far as known) wife before July 12, 1764, when she joined in the conveyance.[36] While a wife or wives unknown to us may, of course, have intervened between the two, Gertrude was probably the mother of his children born down to 1763. Benjamin being mentioned first in the father's will,[38] was presumably older than John III, who, thus the fourth son, by our family records was born in 1753. The eighth of the nine sons, Vantuyle,[38] died Nov. 11, 1829, aged 64; that is, he was born in 1765-6; so he and Richard, the ninth son, and perhaps the seventh son, William, were borne by Charity.

38. T., 15-36, signed Jan. 7, prov. Feb. 27, 1870. Original in "Old Wills" at Newton, Sussex Co. Contemporary copy with Col. H. A. Coursen, Scranton, Pa. In his will John Coursen authorized the completion, after his death, of the sale (T., AK-459) made on June 21, 1772, of 168 8-10 acres (Hull purchase) to Casper Shaver. To his "Beloved wife" (Charity ———) he left the usufruct of his homestead and movable estate, the former, after her death, to be divided among the five younger children, Peter, Abraham, William, VanTuyle and Richard. To his eldest son Jacob, who had already

been set up for himself, he gave the forty acres "where his new house now is," that is, he was then occupying, adjoining the homestead lands (Sussex Deeds, D-309, 315). Isaac, who evidently had also had a portion, was bequeathed five shillings. Benjamin and John were ultimately to share the father's lands, excepting Jacob's 40 acres and the homestead, on payment of £5 each to the five younger brothers on their coming of age.

Of these five younger brothers much might be found in the Sussex and Warren Co. records, but for two only has attempt been made.

ABRAHAM, the sixth son, settled in Wantage to., Sussex Co., some time prior to 1800 (Snell, p. 290). He was already a resident when, in 1790, his wife Jemima joined him in a deed (S. B., 275) conveying some of his late father John's lands near Newton. His homestead (now, 1907, owned by Mr. Ford Margerum) was situated a couple of miles southerly from Deckertown (now "Sussex"), at the more modern "Perry's Mills," between the "Pond" schoolhouse and the "Two Bridges." He established a large and successful tannery (afterward owned by Thomas Teasdale); was ahead of his times in conveying water by aqueduct from a spring to his house; and is recorded in the books of the First Baptist Church of Wantage (commonly known as the Papakating Baptist Church), between his homestead and Deckertown, as a member in 1796, his wife's name appearing as present at meetings. In his will (S. A., 349, 1814) he named his wife Jemima, and, among his children, David, Sarah, George, William, Richard. Search through all neighboring graveyards has failed to discover his tombstone, and it is perhaps one of those fallen, with inscription underneath, in the Papakating (now Deckertown) cemetery, where the contemporary members of his church were buried.

VANTUYLE, the eighth son, arrived in Frankford to., Sussex Co., about 1800 (Snell, p. 392), and founded the hamlet of Coursenville (near another "Papakating," or "Pellettown"), where he resided during his lifetime. Not far away, in the graveyard of the deserted Beemer Church (Congregational), his tombstone shows that Vantile Coursen, a "Deacon of the Congregation," died Nov. 11, 1829, aged 64. Here, too, lie his wife Sally, died Jan. 16, 1847, aged 81; and his sons, Henry D., June 27, 1789—Oct. 3, 1866, and Samuel J., died Nov. 13, 1874, aged 71-3-17, with Hannah A., his wife, died May 14, 1893, aged 86-11-8. Samuel's son, Isaac Vantile Coursen, wife Mary, removed to Colesville, Wantage to., where his family still resides. Of JOHN and his descendants something is

told in the text. Of BENJAMIN it is only known that on Oct. 15th
of the year of his father's death he conveyed (deed with Hon. W. P.
Coursen) part of his inherited lands to William Scholey, and that
by sheriff's deed this reached Casper Shaver's estate in 1774, and
by his heirs was conveyed back to John Coursen III on Jan. 14,
1793 (T., AK-463); and that on June 20, 1778, Benjamin released
to his brother John his share of 180 acres of other inherited lands
(deed with Hon. W. P. Coursen). ISAAC is probably the Isaac
Coursen of Sussex Co. (township not stated, perhaps Hardwick, now
in Warren Co.) for whose estate letters of administration were granted, Feb. 5, 1810, to Mary Coursen, presumably his wife. JACOB,
baptized at Readington on August 14, 1743, was the Jacob of the Mill
of the County Histories. He was born July 30, 1743; married
Mary Nixon (Aug. 9, 1742—April 12, 1828); and died June 5,
1815. These dates have been supplied by his descendant, Mr. Jacob
Allen Coursen, of Branchville, N. J., who could give much information about the Sussex Coursens, especially his own branch. (See
text.)

39. The spellings, "Coursen" and "Coerson," are found in the
record of John I,[5] and the latter in the early days of Jacob Corson's
home, Neshanic (Snell's "Somerset County," p. 785)[21], while the
"son," instead of "sen," was common among both the Staten Island
and Sussex families. The present "Coursen" seems to have been
revived just after Col. John's time. Like the Staten Island "Corson,"
it may be now regarded as the established form.

DICKERSON

[Eliza Drake, wife of Dr. Absalom Woodruff, App. B and Note,
was a granddaughter of Peter Dickerson II, through his dau. Esther,
wife of Col. Jacob Drake, q. v.]

The family history during the Long Island period is especially a
field for further research.

[1]   PHILEMON, b. England, 1598; d. bet. 1665 (will) and 1672
(prob.); m. Mary (1611-77), dau. of Thomas Payne, or
Paine, of Salem, Mass.; was freeman of Salem, 1641; removed to Southold, L. I., 1646-50; freeman of Conn. (while
presumably still of L. I.) 1662. Of their children,

[2]   PETER I, 1648-1721; m. Naomi Mapes (1648-1725). Of
their children,

[3]   THOMAS, 1672-1725; m. Abigail Reeve. Of their children:

[4]   PETER II, b. 1724, at Southold, L. I.; d. May 10, 1780; removed 1745 to Morris Co., N. J., in company with bros. Thomas, Daniel, Joshua, and sister Elizabeth (see tombstone at Morristown); m. (1) Oct. 20, 1745, Ruth Coe (1729—Feb. 14, 1763); (2) Nov. 7, 1763, Sarah Armstrong (1729-98), wid. of John O'Hara. In a paper read before the Washington Association of N. J., the late Hon. Edmund D. Halsey (Drake, Gen. IX) wrote of him: "He was an ardent patriot, and his house in Morristown was, from the beginning of the difficulties with Great Britain, a gathering place of those of kindred mind. He took an active part in awakening and organizing the opposition to the acts of the British Crown, and on the 7th day of January, 1775, was appointed one of the 'Committee of Observation' for Morris County. On the 1st day of May following he was elected a delegate to the Provincial Congress of New Jersey, which met in Trenton the same month. Feb. 7, 1776, he was commissioned Captain of a company (Fifth) in the third battalion of the First Establishment (of the Continental Army), and on the 29th of the November following Captain of a company (First) in the third battalion of the Second Establishment (his men re-enlisting in a body). Both companies he commanded were equipped at his private expense, and the money he so advanced stands to his credit this day at Washington, unpaid."

[5]   Of his eight children by his first wife (of whom Jonathan was the father of Governor and Senator Mahlon Dickerson), ESTHER, March 22, 1757—Oct. 30, 1819; m. (1) Oct. 2, 1774, George KING (1745-80), of Morristown; (2) Dec. 13, 1781, Col. Jacob DRAKE. [For him and their dau. Eliza, w. of Dr. Absalom Woodruff, see Drake and App. B.]

Authorities: As above; Mrs. Edward W. Whelpley (App. B; Gen. XI, 24); Mrs. Eugene T. Gardner (Gen. XII, 49); Savage's Genealogical Dictionary; Early Germans; Stryker; Register; County Histories, etc.

DRAKE

[Eliza, w. of Dr. Absalom Woodruff, App. B and Note, was a dau. of 6 Jacob Drake.]

For Generations 1-5 further research is needed.

[1] ROBERT, b. Devonshire, England, 1580; d. Jan. 4, 1668; moved from Exeter, New England, in 1650, to Hampton, N. H., where, in 1654, he was a selectman.

[2] FRANCIS; Savage says "(supposed to be a son of Robert, although not named in his will), at Portsmouth, N. H., 1661, where he is found on the grand jury, 1663; probably removed to N. J. soon after." Died about 1687 (Middlesex Wills). Sept. 29, 1687, called "Captain" Francis D. of Piscataway (N. J. Archives, Vol. XXIII, p. 182); m. Mary ———. Their son

[3] JOHN; m. (1) Rebecca ——— (and two others, names not known); was a civil magistrate; pastor Baptist Church, Piscataway, N. J., until he d. in 1739. His son

[4] ABRAHAM I; m. Deliverance ———; in 1751 bought land at Drakesville, Mor. Co.; his will is dated 1759, "Roxbury"; (the to. of Drakesville); he d. perhaps 1763. His son,

[5] ABRAHAM II, d. before the date of his father's will of 1759. His son,

[6] JACOB, b. Piscataway, April 21, 1732; d. Sept., 1823; m. (1) Charity Young (1744-76); (2) Esther Dickerson, q. v. He lived at Drakesville, where he owned a large tract of land. The late Hon. Edmund D. Halsey wrote of him (Munsell's Morris Co., p. 25): "At the breaking out of the war he took at once a leading part. He is described as of handsome physique, quick and active in his movements, and of very popular manners. He was Colonel of the Western Battalion of Morris Militia, and resigned his commission to represent the County in the first State Legislature." In 1774-5 he, like his father-in-law, Captain Dickerson, had been appointed one of the "Committee of Observation" (or "Correspondence"), and was a Deputy, May and Sept., 1775, in the Provincial Legislature that was prorogued in December, to be replaced in 1776 by the convention of the "State of New Jersey." His and Esther Dickerson's children were:

[7] CLARISSA H.; m. Dr. Ebenezer WOODRUFF (App. B; Gen. X, 1). JACOB B., b. May 5, 1786. GEORGE KING; Sept. 16, 1788—May 6, 1837; m. Oct. 14, 1815, Mary Alling Halsey (Feb. 13, 1795—April 18, 1872). SILAS, b. April 10, 1790. PETER, b. April 9, 1792.

ELIZA; m. Dr. Absalom WOODRUFF (App. B, Gen. X, 5).

[8]   The children of George King Drake: EDMUND BURKE; Dec. 3, 1817—March 26, 1836; unmarried. ELIZA HALSEY; May 26, 1819—May 23, 1898; m. May 25, 1839, George K. HOWELL (d. Sept., 1851). ANN MACKENZIE; Sept. 19, 1821—Sept. 21, 1880; m. May 25, 1841, Henry Gray DARCY (July 17, 1814—Dec. 19, 20, 1892). MARY LOUISA; Nov. 30, 1823—Jan. 20, 1898; m. May 23, 1847, Judge Edward Wallace SCUDDER (Aug. 12, 1822—Feb. 3, 1893).

[9]   The children of Ann Mackenzie Darcy: MARY; m. Hon. Edmund Drake HALSEY (Sept. 11, 1840—Oct. 17, 1896). ELIZA GRAY; m. Edward Q. KEASBEY. ANNIE. HENRY M.; m. Helen Barklie. JOHN STEVENS. Of Mary Louise Scudder: WALLACE McILVAINE; m. (1) Ida Quimby (deceased); (2) Gertrude Witherspoon. MARY; m. Alexander JAMIESON. LOUISE; m. Capt. Henry P. PERRINE; and three others.

Authorities: As above, and for Dickerson; and "The Combined Registers," First Presb. Church, Morristown, N. J., May, 1883.

MARSH (MENDHAM, N. J.)

[Elizabeth Sophia Coursen, wife of Dr. E. B. Woodruff, Gen. XI, App. B and Note, was a dau. of 5, Hetty Marsh.]

It is an open secret that Mr. John Edward Marsh, of Rahway and N. Y. C., after long and thorough research, has prepared a genealogy of the Marsh family of N. J. that will in due time be made accessible to the public. It would, therefore, not be right to waste time in attempting a duplicate search, so the following is merely a stop-gap for local needs until the standard work appears.

Presumably the Marshes of Mendham are descended from John Marsh, of Hartford, Conn., b. 1618, in Eng., d. 1688, and his wife Ann, dau. of Gov. John Webster; but we have traced back only to

[1]   JOHN MARSH I, of Woodbridge, N. J., who was possibly a son of Samuel Marsh, Sr. (d. 1683), of Elizabethtown. He m. Sarah Clarke. Of their children,

[2]   DANIEL; m. Mary Rolph. Of their children,

[3]   JOHN II, who lived near the mouth of the Rahway River,

N. J.; d. March 9, 1775; m. Elizabeth Dunham. Among their children were

[4] ISAAC; and AMOS, who removed to Mendham and m. Sophia Oliver.

[5] The children of Amos were: FREEMAN. HETTY (Mehitabel); m. Abraham COURSEN (see Coursen, 3; App. B and Note). An old friend of the family has told the writer that when the young gallant from Sussex won her she was the acknowledged "beauty of the county," and any one who remembers her, even in old age, must acknowledge that the judgment was doubtless correct. EPHRAIM; Oct. 1, 1796—Aug. 28, 1864; m. Lavinia, dau. of Joseph W. Heath; an eminent and much respected citizen. JOHN; Oct. 28, 1801— . . .; m. Caroline Hudson (June 27, 1805 —July 27, 1880). OLIVER.

[6] The grandchildren of (4) Isaac were: JOHN EDWARD. WILLIAM LAWRENCE. KATHARINE; m. William Garrett BIBB (deceased). CORDELIA; m. Wilson Cary BIBB (deceased), (son, William Garrett Bibb). For (5) Hetty's children see App. B. Ephraim's were JOSEPH HEATH; Oct. 3, 1819—Feb. 29, 1852; m. Elizabeth (March 26, 1827—March 30, 1892), dau. of Ross Crane. MARY HEATH, b. Aug. 20, 1821; m. Theodore LITTLE; d. w. i., June 15, 1842. JOHN OLIVER; Nov. 2, 1823— June 10, 1852; unmarried. WILLIAM WALLACE; 182(?)—Aug. 30, 1892; m. Ida, dau. of Andrew Reeder. John's were: WILLIAM HUDSON; March 11, 1826-1842; unmarried. HAMPTON OLIVER; July 23, 1831 —Sept. 22, 1894; m. Mary Dayton (Feb. 11, 1837—Sept. 27, 1884); a leading citizen of Morristown. A dau. of (5) Oliver m. Lambert STIGER.

[7] For (5) Hetty's grandchildren, see App. B and Note. The children of (6) Joseph Heath were: MARY HEATH; d. Jan. 27, 1872. MARGARET CRANE. Of William Wallace: CORA LAVINIA; m. Edward J. FOX; two sons. JENNIE AMALIA; m. Dudley IRWIN; four children. EPHRAIM (RAY) REEDER. ETHEL PENN-GAS-KELL; m. Eugene Henry BASKERVILLE. Hampton Oliver's: CAROLINE HUDSON. WILLIAM DAY-TON. JOHN; m. Edith Conyngham; one son. MARY HAMPTON; d. Dec. 28, 1875. HELEN OLIVIA; m.

George Jerome WESLEY. Mrs. Stiger's: MARY S.; m.
—— WILLIAMS; — children. OLIVER MARSH;
m. Angeline ——; two children.

Authorities: Rolph C., son of Christopher Marsh, of Concord,
Penn., through William W. Marsh, Aug. 15, 1872, and, 7, Miss
Margaret C. Marsh; 7, Miss Caroline H. Marsh; Savage; N. J.
Archives; Hatfield; John Marsh, of Hartford, etc., etc.

NEWTON

HANNAH NEWTON was the wife of John WOODRUFFE,
1650-1703 (Gen. VI, App. A), of Southampton, L. I. (Sketch III).
Her brother Benoni was a Town Trustee of that place in 1693 (Note
63). Nothing has been learned of their parentage.

Authorities: Howell, p. 434; Southampton Red Book of Deeds,
folios 77, 78.

RUSSELL

ALICE RUSSEL; m. in 1573, at St. Mary Northgate, Canterbury, Eng., Robert WOODROFFE (d. 1611; of Gen. III), Churchwarden of Fordwich, and Jurat (see Sketch II, Note 15). Nothing
has been learned of her descent.

Authority: Rev. C. E. Woodruff, Notes 5, 13.

STITES

[MARY, wife of Hezekiah Woodruff, 1724-76 (of Gen. VIII,
Sketch IV), was a dau. of 4, John Stites II.]

[1]   JOHN I, b. in England in Cromwell's time; emigrated from
        London to New England, finally settling on Long Island.
        (Littell.)
[2]   RICHARD I; 1640-1702; lived at Hempstead, L. I.
[3]   WILLIAM, b. Hempstead, 1676; d. Springfield, N. J., 1727.
        Of his seven children,
[4]   JOHN II, b. at Hempstead, 1706; d. at Springfield, N. J.,
        1782. As already told (Sketch IV), he was a Chosen Free-
        holder and Justice of Elizabethtown, and a Deputy in the
        Provincial Congress of New Jersey in 1775. His tombstone
        at Springfield tells us that he "lived beloved and died la-

mented by Church and State." He m. (1) Abigail Rushmore; (2) Margaret Hampton (1715-84). His children
were:

[5]   By (1), HEZEKIAH (Notes 114, 116). MARY; m. Heze-
kiah WOODRUFF (Sketch IV). By (2), SARAH; m.
Rev. John GANO. MARGARET; m. Rev. James MAN-
NING, Prest. Brown University, Providence, R. I. ABI-
GAIL; m. Isaac WOODRUFF (Note 107). JOHN; m.
in N. Y.; returned to Elizabethtown; went West. RICH-
ARD II was b. 1747; m. Sarah Dennis (Littell says Sarah
Thompson); Captain First Battalion, Somerset, Feb. 9,
1776; Captain, Colonel Hunt's battalion, "Heard's Brigade," July 5, 1776; resigned July, 1776; Captain, Col.
Thompson's battalion "Detached Militia" (Stryker); d.
(from wounds received Aug. 27th at the battle of Long
Island) on Sept. 16, 1776, as by his tombstone, removed
from St. John's Church, Elizabethtown, to Morristown,
N. J. Having d. first, his father's will (T. 23-426) does
not name him, but as "my grandson Richard Stites," does
name his son.

[6]   RICHARD (III) MONTGOMERY, b. 1777; d. in Savannah, Ga., about 1815. His son, Judge   .

[7]   RICHARD (IV) WAYNE, b. in Savannah, Ga., Nov. 24,
1802; removed to Morristown, N. J. He and the father of
the writer more than once talked in the latter's hearing
of the connection between our two families, through the
marriage of Hezekiah and (5) Mary. He m. Elizabeth
Cooke (April 6, 1806—Feb. 29, 1896), and d. July 2, 1777;
the ancestor of many honored citizens of our State.

Authorities: Mrs. William B. Beekman; Cortland Parker, Jr.,
Esquire; Littell; Hatfield, etc.

WICK

[Mary, wife of Dr. H. S. Woodruff, Sketch V, was a granddaughter of Henry Wick, through his dau. Mary, wife of Dr. E. Blachly.]
[1]   JOHN; 1661—Jan. 16, 1719; was first recorded in the Southampton, L. I., Town Records at date of April 4, 1693, when
he was granted a site for a fulling mill on the "Streame of
the Little River called by the name of peaconnuck": and
thereafter "Mr. John Wick," or "Justice Wick," Sheriff of

Suffolk Co., 1699-1700 and 1701-2, and a magistrate until his death, had a fair share of mention as a "man of importance in his day" (Pelletreau S. T. R., Vol. III, p. 27). He removed to the neighboring Bridge Hampton, where he d., and at his own request was bur. on his own land. No evidence has been found to connect him with Joseph Wickham, of Sagg (Howell, 441), or to imply that, as has been alleged, his name was "Wickham," not "Wick." He had a wife Temperance, and children, Job, John (Yale, B.A., 1722), Henry, Samuel, Daniel, James, Temperance, Ann, Phebe, Edith.

[2]   HENRY; Oct. 23, 1707—Dec. 21, 1780; m. 1725, Mary Cooper, q. v.; and in 1737 was living near Bridge Hampton, on the way to Sagg (S. T. R., III, p. 63). In 1746 Nathan Cooper, of Roxbury (Chester) to., and Henry Wick, of "Suffolk Co., L. I.," jointly bought 1,114 acres on the Passaic, and in 1748 Cooper released his half to Henry Wick, of "Morristown, N. J." (Mor. H-122, B-142), so he doubtless came here between the two dates. With later purchases the "Wick tract" came to measure over 1,400 acres, and has become widely known through the wintering (1780-81) on it, and near by, of our Revolutionary army; while Miss Tempe's rescue of her pet saddle horse has added interest to the old house (still standing in 1908) in which she so successfully hid it. [Ill. G, 12, 11; Ill. H; it was nearly in front of Dr. Leddell's house that she refused to give up her pet to our disorderly soldiers and galloped away from them.] The father was Captain of a company of Morris Co. cavalry that did good service in the war, and engaged in at least one sharp fight, though frequently detailed as guard for Gov. Livingston and the Privy Council (Munsell's Mor. Co., p. 35; search for further evidence is kindly being made at the Adjutant-General's office, Trenton).

    "Daniel," "John," and other Wicks, recorded in the Presbyterian Church Register here, would seem, from their names, to have also been descendants of Henry's father. Henry's children were:

[3]   HENRY; March 9, 1737—Sept. 10, 1781; m. Feb. 7, 1760, Elizabeth Cooper (1746—Feb. 1, 1782); children, Mary (Tuttle) and Chloe. MARY; Aug. 13, 1739—Sept. 18, 1786; m. June 19, 1758 (5), Dr. Ebenezer BLACHLY

III, q. v.; ancestress of many Woodruffs, Blachlys, and others. JAMES; Dec. 19, 1741; not m. PHEBE; Nov. 9, 1746—June 15, 1806; m. April 5, 1770, Dr. William LEDDELL II (App. E). TEMPE; Oct. 30, 1758—April 28, 1822; m. Captain William TUTTLE (previously private in Capt. Dickerson's company, Third Battalion, Second Establishment, Continental Army; Nov. 5, 1760—Jan. 11, 1836). As well as her sister Phebe, she was an ancestress of Blachlys. See (7) Joseph Warren Blachly.

Authorities: Miss Mary E. Leddell; Mrs. C. C. Davis; Howell; S. T. R.; Register; Munsell's Mor. Co., etc.

APPENDIX E

LEDDELL

[Note 118; Note to App. B; Sketch V; Map 11.]

Although not in the direct line, as neighbors, friends, and kin (through Phebe, dau. of Henry and Mary Cooper Wick, App. D), the Leddells were of the family group at Washington Corner.

[1]   WILLIAM I, M.D., was a French naval surgeon "of the high seas" (by tradition from Alsace), stationed at Cuba, who resigned from the service and settled in New Jersey (Wickes). He m. (1) Louise ——— (son John; nothing known of him); (2) Esther Nightingale. Mrs. C. C. (Sara Leddell) Davis (5), who has been very kind in supplying valuable information, writes that in the four old deeds in her possession, dating from Feb. 15, 1751, to Feb. 10, 1761, his name is given as William Leddel, Gent., Dr. W. L., and W. L., Physician; his residence as Morris Co. and the Borough of Elizabeth (he is believed to have owned lands near New Providence). He d. in June, 1762. On May 5, 1767, his son,

[2]   WILLIAM II, M.D. (1747—Aug., 1827), by the advice of his guardian, John Carl, Esquire, became a pupil of Dr. Ebenezer Blachly, of Mendham, "to learn the art of physic and surgery." On Thursday, April 5, 1770, he m. Phebe (Nov. 9, 1746—June 15, 1806), dau. of Henry Wick (App. D); was energetic and distinguished; a skillful botanist; successful in his large practice and in business, having helped supply the Revolutionary soldiers camped near by; was one of the first Sheriffs of Morris Co., serving two terms; is recorded (Stryker, p. 663) as a private in the Morris Co. militia; was a Major in the "Whiskey Insurrection" (1794), and a Captain of cavalry in the War of 1812; his military papers are with the N. J. Hist. Society. Their children were:

[3]   WILLIAM III (Sept. 2, 1772—Mar. 23, 1780).   MARY

124

(Feb. 3, 1774—May 5, 1780). HENRY, M.D. (Sept. 16, 1776—Jan. 30, 1799); m. Margaret McVicker (dau. Phebe, m. George Dayton; one son). TEMPERANCE (Aug. 25, 1779—Jan. 18, 1810); m. Dr. Philip McCREA (dau. Tempe, m. Geo. H. Thompson). ELIZA (Oct. 11, 1781—Dec. 23, 1803); m. Dr. William HAMPTON (1781-1816), w. i. MARY TAILOR (Nov. 20, 1786—Sept. 7, 1857); m. John LATHAM [dau. Caroline, m. (1) Dr. Fred'k PERRY, 2 children; m. (2) Halleck VANCE]. JOHN WICK, M.D.; Oct. 25, 1783—April 15, 1865; ed. Ezra Fairchild School (Note 147); studied med. with his father, and licensed at 18; at 21 m. Jemima (June 1, 1780—Feb. 25, 1866), youngest dau. of Samuel Wills (see Cooper); practiced very successfully at Washington Corner, Mendham (until 1833) and Ralston (or Roxiticus; see Note to App. B, Absalom Woodruff), where he bought the farm and mill of John Ralston, now occupied by Mrs. DeMott (5). He was highly esteemed as physician, business man and citizen. His children were:

[4] WILLIAM, b. Nov. 20, 1806; m. Mary Emily Halsey, who d. Aug. 22, 1888. FRANCES, b. Aug. 27, 1808; m. Rev. Jonas DENTON (1807-88). SAMUEL WILLS, M.D.; Aug. 9, 1810—July 15, 1875; studied med. with his father, but preferring business and farming, did not practice; Union College, B.A. about 1831; m. (1) Margaret Horton, who d. 1847; (2) Emma Louisa Halsey (May 5, 1817—Sept. 6, 1891). TEMPE, b. Sept. 30, 1812; d. Oct. 18, 1848; m. George W. SEWARD. SARAH E., b. April 30, 1815; m. Charles STARR. MARY HENRIETTA, b. July 26, 1822; m. Gen. Nathan A. COOPER (April 29, 1802—July 22, 1872).

[5 and 6] William's children were: JOHN. JOHN WICK; m. Caroline Sergent (two children); d. Mar. 13, 1892. MARY ELIZABETH. CHARLES STARR; m. Lizzie Murphy. Frances Denton's children were: AUGUSTA. JOHN L.; m. Jennie Melick. MARY. SARAH; m. Hamilton RODDIS (two children). Samuel Wills and Margaret Horton's children were: MARGARET MARIA; m. Peter DEMOTT. WILLIAM JOHN; m. Ida Alexander (two children). Samuel and Emma Louisa Halsey's children were: SARA TEMPE; m. Calvin C. DAVIS. SAMUEL FRED-

ERICK; m. Marian W. Maxwell. Tempe Seward's children were: WILLIAM HENRY; never married. SARAH C.; d. a missionary in India. Rev. SAMUEL S.; m. Christiana Kimber (deceased). GEORGE FREDERICK (late our Consul-General at Shanghai, and Minister at Peking, China; President, Fidelity and Casualty Co., N. Y. C.); m. Katharine Sherman. JOHN L.; m. Lydia Kimber. Sarah E. Starr's children were: LOUISA; AUGUSTUS; MARY ELLEN. Mary Henrietta Cooper's children were: ANNA E. BEULAH; m. Henry DAYTON. MARY; m. E. Irvin SMITH. TILLIE R. LAURA H.; m. Oscar BABBITT. NATHAN; m. —— Fisher. ABRAHAM; m. Mary Turner.

Authorities: Miss M. E. Leddell (5); Mrs. C. C. Davis (5); and others; Wickes; County Histories, etc.

INDEX

TO THE SKETCHES AND NOTES

This index does not include references to the appendices. Where a person indexed is the subject of one of the five sketches, all mention of his name on the pages of that sketch is denoted by I, II, III, etc.

A single given name or surname in the index may refer to more than one individual.

The names of kings, dukes, "authorities," etc., that are not essential to the narrative, are generally omitted from the index.

Names of places are indexed only for pages on which information is given about them, and only places of comparative importance to the narrative are included.

INDEX TO WOODRUFFS.

INDEX OF PERSONS OTHER THAN WOODRUFF.

INDEX OF PLACES.

INDEX OF SUBJECTS.

CPSIA information can be obtained
at www.ICGtesting.com
Printed in the USA
LVOW04s2013130218

566499LV00012B/47/P

9 781276 990899